"You never know when you will suddenly be confronted by a 'do or die' situation. None of us can. Jason's unique collection of such incidents are recounted by real CIA covert operations officers. And intriguing and fascinating as they are, their greatest value is in giving you insight into the way of thinking and reacting that these covert operators demonstrate. Just one story could save your life."

—Peter Earnest, executive director of the International Spy Museum and former CIA clandestine service officer

"In the past fifty years, I have conducted leadership development workshops for over 100,000 leaders in Russia, Europe, the United States, Mexico, Canada, and Australia. I can confirm that whether you travel around the world or just in the United States, this is a must-have book for surviving in today's world. Every American can benefit from this book and it should be mandatory reading for staying safe."

—Peter A. Land, Colonel USAF (Ret.), former director of management consultation, United States Air Force

"*Survive Like a Spy* is both a thrilling read and a primer full of lifesaving tactics. It's a rare chance you get to learn from the best CIA operatives on how to stay alive in the crazy world we live in, which is why I highly recommend this book."

—Alain Burrese, former Army sniper and author of *Survive a Shooting*

"As someone who's worked operations with the CIA, I can tell you that Jason and his team are the real deal and that you'll absolutely learn many life-saving skills in this book. In fact, I can't believe the CIA let Jason share some of these stories."

—Cade Courtley, former Navy SEAL and author of *Seal Survival Guide*

"I attest to the life-saving techniques presented in this book. I have relied on the tradecraft skills disclosed in this book to keep me alive and out of foreign prisons. I have conducted operations with the operatives who have shared their stories in this book, and as amazing as it sounds, this book presents factual and accurate methods used by intelligence operatives."
—Michael D., former clandestine operations officer,
CIA, NSA, DIA

"*Survive Like a Spy* is an incredible survival book. Even though I'm a Marine, retired police officer, and black belt, I learned spy survival tricks that I can add to my arsenal."
—Danny Lane, ninth degree black belt master and
founder of the World Martial Arts Centers and
the World Martial Arts Federation

"Great tips on staying safe from a former CIA officer. This book is a good addition to the library of anyone who wants to keep themselves and their families out of trouble."
—Colonel Scott Hovis, United States Army

Praise for Jason Hanson

"When I first met Jason Hanson while he was pitching me his business on *Shark Tank*, I knew that his company was going to be a winner—and more importantly that I might learn some tips that could one day save my life!"
—Daymond John, star of ABC's *Shark Tank*

"Jason Hanson has forgotten more tradecraft than most will ever know."
—Rorke Denver, Navy SEAL and *New York Times*
bestselling author of *Damn Few*

SURVIVE LIKE A SPY

Real CIA Operatives Reveal How
They Stay Safe in a Dangerous World
and How You Can Too

JASON HANSON

A TarcherPerigee Book

tarcherperigee

an imprint of Penguin Random House LLC
penguinrandomhouse.com

First trade paperback edition 2020

TarcherPerigee with tp colophon is a registered trademark of Penguin Random House LLC.

Most TarcherPerigee books are available at special quantity discounts for bulk purchase for sales promotions, premiums, fund-raising, and educational needs. Special books or book excerpts also can be created to fit specific needs. For details, write: SpecialMarkets@penguinrandomhouse.com.

ISBN (hardcover) 9780143131595
ISBN (e-book) 9781524705251
ISBN (paperback) 9780143131601

Printed in the United States of America

ScoutAutomatedPrintCode

Book design by Sabrina Bowers

DEDICATION

This book is dedicated to my wife Amanda and our kids.
(I'm not going to name our kids because
I'm not sure which ones we're going to keep.)

CONTENTS

INTRODUCTION: WELCOME TO THE REAL WORLD OF
CIA OPERATIVES   ix

CHAPTER ONE: SPY SENSE
Do You Have What It Takes to Be a Spy?   1

CHAPTER TWO: WHEN ONE MISSION BECOMES TWO
Using Cover Stops, Hunker-Down Sites, and Secret Caches
to Spy on a Terrorist Cell   17

CHAPTER THREE: DR. X AND THE PUFFER FISH
How Secret Signals, Covert Communication, and a
Five-Hour Surveillance Detection Route Saved America
from a Deadly Biological Weapon   41

CHAPTER FOUR: GATHERING INTELLIGENCE IN A WAR ZONE
Surviving Bombings and Brutality During a Civil War
in El Salvador   61

CHAPTER FIVE: STEALING A TOP-SECRET HOLOGRAM
FROM THE RUSSIANS
How to Get Anyone to Do What You Want   83

CHAPTER SIX: SNATCHING AND GRABBING A NARCO-TERRORIST
How to Survive a Kidnapping   113

CHAPTER SEVEN: PROTECTING THE GREATEST MINDS IN THE
WORLD FROM HOSTILE FOREIGN COUNTRIES

How to Travel Safely When Others Want to Harm You   139

CHAPTER EIGHT: TURNING A SOLDIER INTO A SPY

How a First-Time Case Officer Taught a Decorated War Hero
to Do Brush Passes, Dead Drops, and Signaling to Help the
United States   161

CHAPTER NINE: GIVING A HIGH-LEVEL AMBASSADOR A BUGGED
PAINTING

How to Embed Cameras and Microphones When It's *You*
Who Needs to Spy on Someone   179

CHAPTER TEN: THE SPY WHO SOLD CHINA COMPUTERS
SECRETLY INFECTED WITH MALWARE

How CIA Officers Avoid Being Hacked, Spied On, or
Scammed   197

CHAPTER ELEVEN: TAKING CONTROL

What You Can Do Right Now to Lead a Secure Life and
Survive Anything from Blackouts to Economic Collapses
to Home Invasions   217

Glossary of Spy Terms   235

References   239

Acknowledgments   241

About the Author   243

INTRODUCTION

Welcome to the Real World of CIA Operatives

In the world where I'm about to take you, everything might appear completely ordinary . . . *at first.*

At a fine French restaurant in a big city, two academic types are sharing an elaborate meal and an expensive bottle of wine. They're both wearing nice suits and appear polished and sophisticated. They might be chatting about their research or celebrating a promotion.

On a sweltering hot day in a city in southern Asia, an American tourist casually poses in front of a fountain while his taxi driver snaps a couple of quick pictures. The tourist gets back into the taxi and waits patiently in the heat for the traffic to thin out just like everyone else.

There's nothing particularly out of the ordinary about the two scenarios I've just outlined—a couple of professors sharing a meal, and a tourist posing for a picture. Chances are, if you were passing by you wouldn't have noticed anything strange about either of these situations. But in the real world of spies, things aren't always what they seem. If you were trained in the art of espionage tradecraft you might have picked up on a few curious details. For example, it's a bit odd that the tourist got out of the taxi to pose for a picture in the middle of a traffic jam—especially since there was nothing at all remarkable about that fountain. What's actually more interesting is the building behind the fountain. If you looked more closely, you would see that it is under the protection of heavily armed guards.

There's something different about those two academics too. If you had been sitting in the park just a few blocks from the restaurant, you may have noticed one of them strolling through on his way to dinner. If you were paying attention, you might have seen him slow down just slightly as he passed by a particular bench. It's unlikely you would have caught it because he's been well trained, but he quickly scanned the side of the bench looking for a small tack. It wasn't there, so that meant the meeting with his case officer was still on and he proceeded to the restaurant.

In my previous book, *Spy Secrets That Can Save Your Life*, I showed how the simple tactics I learned as a CIA officer could help regular Americans lead safer and more secure lives.

This time I'm going to take you much deeper into the world of espionage. I'm blessed to have an excellent team of former CIA officers (there is nobody else I'd want by my side during an operation), and these incredibly brave men and women have worked dangerous missions all over the world and we owe them a huge debt of gratitude. The stories you are about to hear are as thrilling as anything you'd read in a spy novel, but that's not all. You're also going to see how CIA operatives use their skills and finely honed instincts to survive everything from clandestine operations in hostile foreign countries to bombings in brutal war zones. These highly trained individuals have put everything on the line to ensure America's safety. They have recruited spies, extracted secrets from our enemies, and evaded capture from foreign police. And now you're going to learn how these same tactics that have been used in the field by real intelligence officers can help keep you and your family safe. You're going to learn some exciting and potentially life-saving skills, including:

- How to survive a kidnapping.
- How to increase your chances of surviving an IED (improvised explosive device) attack.
- How cover stops and hunker-down sites can keep a potential terrorist (or criminal) from following you home.
- What tasking means, and how to get someone to accept it.
- The number one way to deal with a threatening individual.
- How to run an SDR (surveillance detection route) like a pro—to ensure the safety of you and your family.
- How to improvise a weapon using ordinary, inexpensive items you may already have at home.
- The critical items you need to take with you while traveling in the age of terrorism.
- How to create covert communications signals to protect your family.

HOW I WROTE THIS BOOK

As I mentioned, I'm incredibly grateful for the men and women of the CIA and I assured everyone that I would protect their privacy. As you might imagine, privacy is of the utmost importance to those working in the intelligence field. For this reason, all names and identifying details have been changed, and the stories have been edited for clarity and to ensure they would be understandable to people who do not work in the intelligence field. In some instances, dates and/or geographical regions have been changed. Again, this was critical to do to ensure the privacy of everyone who joined me in this book.

MY MISSION: A SAFER, HAPPIER, AND MORE SUCCESSFUL LIFE

My mission with everything I do is to keep finding new ways to help you live a safer, happier, and more successful life. This is why I wrote this book and why I started the Spy Escape & Evasion training company that has saved numerous lives and shared spy secrets with tens of thousands of people (www.SpyEscape.com).

It is my hope that what you're about to read will entertain you, but also help you to feel empowered and more prepared. Whether you live in rural America, the suburbs, or near a major metropolitan area, it is my hope that you will continue to enjoy your life, and can move forward with your work, leisure activities, and travel plans, even as the world grows more complicated and feels more dangerous than ever before. I'm honored to help you expand your arsenal of skills, and I'm committed to helping you feel more confident in your ability to keep you and your family safe in any situation.

CHAPTER ONE

SPY SENSE

Do You Have What It Takes to Be a Spy?

HOW THE CYCLE WORKS

Imagine the following scenario:

You and your wife are invited to a dinner party at a neighbor's house. If you were being completely honest, you're not exactly excited about going. Maybe you were up late with the kids, or you have a big project due at work in a couple of days. It feels like you've been to parties like this a thousand times. You spend the evening chatting with the other guests about typical topics such as what sports your kids are playing or upcoming vacation plans. But then you meet SEBASTIAN,* who is new to the area. He's friendly and fun to talk to, and is fascinated to know you're a researcher at "Company X." It turns out he's a consultant for "Company Y." You talk about what you do for a bit, and he's very familiar with your area of expertise. You're impressed by how smart he is and it's refreshing to find someone who is interested in your work. He suggests meeting for lunch to talk more, and you happily agree. SEBASTIAN suggests an extravagant lunch

---

* In official documents pertaining to espionage activity, aliases are always written in all caps.

spot, a place you've always wanted to go, but the cost isn't really in your budget. You talk about your work for a while—he has interesting questions and seems genuinely curious about what you do, especially related to your role on Project Y. The conversation flows, and you find out that you're both avid tennis players. SEBASTIAN asks if you're a member of X Tennis Club. You confess you've never been, you can't manage the dues while paying a mortgage and saving for the kids' college. SEBASTIAN says he'd be happy to have you as his guest. You make a date to play tennis, and SEBASTIAN insists on picking up the check.

At work later that week, there's a new development with Project Y, and you remember SEBASTIAN had been curious about that. He's been a great guy so far, buying lunch and offering to take you to his club, and so you decide to call him up and tell him about it. You're glad you did, because he seems so happy with the information—and it feels good to be helpful. The relationship continues and you and SEBASTIAN become better friends. You enjoy his company, he's fun to play tennis with, and is always up for a good meal. You also appreciate his interest in your work and you start to keep him updated on things. It turns out the information you have helps him out so much that he got you a small consulting fee. It really takes some pressure off to have extra money to put away for the kids' college.

When there's a bigger change with Project Y, and you tell him about it, your fee suddenly doubles. Now you can save for college *and* afford that tennis club you've always wanted to join. Your wife is thrilled, and the extra money is incredibly handy. This continues on for a while, and even though you love the extra money and enjoy SEBASTIAN's company, you have moments when you wonder if you should be giving SEBASTIAN this information; what's he doing with it? But you really don't want to give up the money, especially since your wife has started redoing your kitchen. SEBASTIAN has been a good friend, and is so knowledgeable about Y already, surely it doesn't matter that you're throwing him a bit more information? It's not hurting anyone, right?

If all of that seems too good to be true—the friendship, the money, the tennis club—you're right. SEBASTIAN has expertly spotted someone with access, found his vulnerabilities, developed him, and recruited him to be a spy.

SPIES ARE THE BEST SALESPEOPLE IN THE WORLD

What do spies really do? They recruit people who have information that the U.S. government feels can be beneficial to our national security. The United States might learn that a foreign government is developing a dangerous weapon and we need to learn more about it to keep our citizens safe. Or maybe we suspect a terrorist cell is planning to harm Americans. In that case we might need to infiltrate a foreign country to gather boots-on-the-ground information so we can stop the threat.

Or, as a former intelligence officer who worked for many years as a case officer puts it:

"We're salesmen. We're just selling a different product, and that product is treason."

As you might imagine, treason is not an easy product to sell. Case officers are highly trained in the art of clandestine HUMINT asset recruiting. HUMINT is simply any information that can be gathered from human sources. Case officers recruit people who live or work in a foreign country to be spies for the U.S. government. The cycle that case officers routinely use follows a progression of spotting, assessing potential recruits, development, and then recruitment. Once the individual is recruited, he or she is officially known as an "agent" and works closely with the case officer to provide information for the

United States in return for some sort of compensation. If you're thinking that being an agent sounds a lot like being a spy, you're absolutely right. While "agent" is the official term used in espionage, the bottom line is that "agent" is just a more technical term for "spy." So both the CIA officer and the person recruited are spies.

SPOTTING: WHO ARE WE LOOKING FOR?

How exactly does a regular person end up committing treason against their home country and spying for the U.S. government? Who are we looking for? Does this person have any particular skills? If you think the United States is looking for someone who is great with a firearm and can easily handle a wild car chase, you're mistaken. The right agent is going to have a few essential qualities, but the number one thing a case officer is looking for in an agent is a person with *access*. The potential agent must have a connection to someone who has information that the U.S. government cannot get on its own. Without access, there's no point. As you'll soon see, academics and researchers often possess very valuable information about chemicals, weapons, computer programs, and encryption systems that different countries want to get their hands on. In that case, these people have access to valuable information. A person may also be desirable because they have access to technology. It's also possible that a case officer will recruit someone because they have relationships with certain high-level individuals. They may be close friends with a diplomat, or with someone who works in the military. People who can travel freely between one country and a "hostile" country may also have access. They can spend time in a country the United States cannot easily explore, and can pick up information and bring it back.

ASSESSING A RECRUIT

A case officer has found someone with excellent access to power players who have information the United States wants. That's a great start, but it's not enough. Any potential recruit must be assessed before the cycle moves forward. It must be determined that the person being assessed isn't under surveillance from his own country, and isn't working for that country's counterintelligence. The potential recruits who are thought to be the highest risk are the ones that defect—who show up at the American embassy offering to give information in exchange for being allowed asylum in the United States. Extra precautions must be taken to make sure that this person wasn't sent by his own country, pretending to want asylum.

Other risks also have to be ruled out, such as is the person likely able to handle the challenges of the job? Will they be able to handle the training? Will they be able to master basic tradecraft such as signaling, brush passes, and dead drops? In a best-case scenario, any agent we recruit will be reasonable and calm. Obviously, spying is dangerous and can have huge consequences, ranging from jail time to execution. If the agent is reasonable and easy to deal with, there's a better chance that they won't get caught. Unfortunately, rational people aren't always the ones who decide to become spies. Money problems, revenge, and anger are sometimes reasons a person decides to spy for the United States. A person who is motivated by these things might be less trustworthy and harder to handle—and therefore much more likely to get caught.

DEVELOPING AND RECRUITING

In the stories that follow, we'll go in-depth into the development-and-recruiting cycle. When a case officer develops an asset, he's doing everything in his power to develop a good rapport and set up a scenario where the asset feels comfortable sharing secrets. As one of my CIA buddies likes to say, "I know I'm developing someone properly when he feels I'm the only person in the world who truly understands him, and that's when he's ready to be officially recruited." Once an agent is recruited, he's an actual witting spy for the U.S. government, and that's when the big challenges (and fun and excitement) really begin.

ONE OF THE MOST COMMON REASONS PEOPLE AGREE TO SELL THEIR COUNTRY'S SECRETS TO THE UNITED STATES

There are many reasons a person might decide to sell their country's secrets to the United States. Money is an obvious reason. Having large debts or not enough money to get by on can put people in a desperate situation. Some people are looking to add a sense of excitement to their lives, or they share a strong personal philosophy with the United States. It's also possible they are hoping to obtain a visa into the United States for themselves or their family. But if you ask a bunch of spies what the number one reason is, you're going to get an answer that just might surprise you. Education. One of the most attractive carrots to dangle in the espionage game is the promise of a fully funded top-notch education for a recruit's son or daughter at one of America's finest colleges or universities.

THE ELEMENTS OF SPY SENSE

Once you've lived the inside-out world of espionage, you never shed it. It's a mentality, a double standard of existence.

—JOHN LE CARRÉ

Thanks to Hollywood, it's easy to assume that espionage is all about surviving in enemy territories or escaping from potentially deadly situations—like a gunfight or even jumping out of a helicopter. The picture that Hollywood paints suggests that what makes a spy good at his job is just physical strength and years of special training. Of course, intelligence officers are highly trained individuals who are probably more capable of defending themselves (or someone else) than just about anyone else in the world. But when it comes to espionage, your ability to survive a knife fight or escape from a foreign captor is only one small part of the package. Intelligence officers all possess something I call "spy sense." Spy sense is a complex mix of traits that allows a spy to develop a potential asset and recruit individuals to share their country's secrets, as well as know how to survive in the most extreme and dangerous situations imaginable. While all intelligence officers have their own special touches they bring to their craft, ultimately they share "spy sense" as a core foundation.

SPY TRAIT # 1: THE RIGHT MIND-SET

MAX: None of my training matters if I'm not in the right frame of mind. Even though we have the absolute best training available, none of it really matters if you don't have the right mind-set. Spies need to have a huge amount of faith to do what they do. I don't mean the religious kind of faith, though I suppose that could help. First, you have to have absolute faith in the mission you are about to take on. I worked on a lot of "hard targets" [a hard target is an operation that someone else has tried before, but failed] during the course of my career, and I've done things that on the surface might sound frightening. I've worked operations where I've had to snatch-and-grab major narco-terrorists . . . I've had to break into hotel rooms. You never know what's going to be required of you, but it can be extreme, and if you don't have faith in the actual mission and what the mission is for, you're not going to be able to do it. If I'm breaking into some guy's hotel room to take something, I need to feel convinced that what I'm doing is for the greater good and the cause makes it worth it. If I don't feel this way, I might not apply myself a hundred percent, and that's a recipe for a failed mission. If I believe in the underlying cause, I'll do whatever it takes to get the job done.

> If I believe in the underlying cause, I'll do whatever it takes to get the job done.

And I know from experience that that could be almost anything.

Faith in Yourself and Your Ability

Second, you have to have an extreme amount of faith in your-self. Things aren't always cut-and-dry; you can't plan every-thing in advance. Obviously planning is essential, but you can't plan for every outcome, like locked doors or fences where you don't want them. You have to have faith that you'll figure out what to do no matter what happens. Sometimes it's hard to make other people involved in operations understand this.

Once I'm in the right mind-set, I know deep down that nothing will stop me. I was once involved in an operation that required me to break into an apartment in a foreign city. This had to be done delicately—I couldn't just bust in and get what we needed. I needed to slip in and out without anyone knowing I was ever there. I knew I could do it, but during the planning stages I just didn't know how.

There are many different ways to tackle obstacles like this. It's possible I'd be able to break in through the front door or window. It's also possible that I'd bribe someone who has a key to let me in or to copy it. Maybe I'd talk my way in somehow. I had no doubts that I could do it. But the guys planning the operation aren't always comfortable with that level of unknown. It took much convincing on my part that, even though I didn't have a plan in place, I'd be able to get the job done once I was there. That's the level of faith I'm talking about: faith that anything can happen, and you'll always be ready to tackle it one way or another.

SPY TRAIT #2: SPIES ARE EMPATHETIC

ALEX: I'm good at what I do because I use a combo of street savvy, kindness, and empathy—and that's pretty much the opposite of how I was taught to do it at the Farm. It might sound strange to say that empathy plays a role in spying. After all, we are all well aware that many times we've met the people we're recruiting while working a cover and pretending to be someone we aren't. I'll also admit that when I'm recruiting someone I'm actively doing everything I can to exploit his or her vulnerabilities. Once I put a finger on someone's vulnerability, I do everything I can to massage it—really work it. If I'm recruiting someone who indicates he feels insecure about his career, I'll probably tell him how impressed I am by what he does. Then I'll ask him lots of questions about his job, showing how interested I am. I'll be hanging on every word— really showing him that I'm anxious to hear more. I also know that none of this would work if I didn't care about the person I was trying to recruit. (And by the way, no one is ever forced or threatened to spy for the U.S. government.) The case officer/ agent relationship, while unusual, is something you slowly let grow over time, and a genuine connection is made. Any agent you recruit is going to know if a case officer doesn't care about him or his safety. They'll also know if you are just looking to get information and then throw them aside. That's seduction for seduction's sake and it doesn't work. Everyone I've recruited is a person—and each one has had many wonderful qualities . . . and yes, that includes access to information, but they are doing great things for our country. You can't ever forget that.

SPY TRAIT #3: NO MATTER WHAT YOU SEE, YOU DON'T SHOW FEAR

MICHELLE: I have traveled all over the world . . . I've been to the Congo, New Delhi, Kathmandu, and Iran, to name a few. I learned early on that you have to pay attention to everything that's going on around you, and no matter what you see, you don't show fear. Knowledge is power, and that's what I had to learn in order to be really good at my job. I'd try to know more about the enemy than they knew about me. It's the only way to succeed. Every day you work to learn something new, and that helps you to expand as a case officer. There were many situations when I felt fear. I'd take a deep breath, and tell myself not to think about what I'd be doing in an hour, but to pay attention to what was going on now. Ultimately, while I became more attuned to fear when I was working for the Agency, the truth is, it's not really that different than any fear I might have felt in high school or college. Those times when you did something silly like stay out late and realize you have no way to get home and you don't have any money. You feel that fear, but you figure it out, and you learn a lesson. You never make the same mistake again, or you learn to have a backup plan. Espionage isn't so different: You embrace the fear in those situations and take charge. You accept the fear and even learn to embrace it. I also learned to accept that, to some extent, I have no control. Obviously I had my training, my smarts, and there were plans—but once you accept that there are some things you can't control, it helps. I grew up in a very mountainous area, and I think this taught me something. I would wake up, look out my window, and think, "Those mountains look angry today." It was simple, really—the mountains had such power. I had no control. I never forgot that.

SPY TRAIT #4: SPIES ARE SOCIAL PEOPLE

SARAH: Clan-ops [clandestine operations] is not for the faint of heart or the optimist. You need to think about what can go wrong and know there's a good chance it will go wrong. Clan-ops requires pragmatism, an unwavering determination, and a healthy dose of ego. An intelligence officer looking to recruit foreign agents willing to share their country's secrets with the United States is going to have to be comfortable meeting with other people—in very different settings. An intelligence officer might meet a possible recruit at a café frequented by locals, at a university, or even at a dinner at a diplomat's home. This means having enough confidence to talk to a person who might dabble with some of the darker elements of his country, as well as the ultra-rich and powerful at a society event. Since spies are sent to recruit others and convince them to share state secrets over a period of time, a spy has to be instantly likable. Others need to be comfortable talking to you and feel an innate ability to trust you.

You Must Be a Team Player

You also need to be a team player. Espionage is truly a people business. Everyone you work with—the director of operations, the analysts, the people creating your materials—you are all part of a team, and each member brings their own unique skills and expertise to the table. It's hugely important to remember that. It's never one individual who is responsible for the outcome of the operation.

> **Espionage is truly a people business.**

SPY TRAIT #5: SPIES UNDERSTAND THAT MANIPULATING PEOPLE IS PART OF THE JOB

CORMAC: Some of my colleagues in the intelligence world prefer to think, "Spies are persuasive," but that's not accurate. Spies need to be manipulative, and that's different. The ability to manipulate a person, to get him to do what you want while thinking it's actually what he wants, makes the difference between succeeding and not succeeding. I think it's more than selling him something—it's getting him to accept and want what you're selling. Of course, there are ways to do this officially, it's all written down and codified, and there are guidelines about how to do it, but you can't recruit someone without being able to get into his head and find out what makes him tick. You have to trick him and manipulate him. When I'm developing a guy, I always say that I'll pay him for nursery rhymes. I don't care what it is he's giving me. I want control. So if he comes to me with nursery rhymes I'll give him money. Now he's getting comfortable with the extra hundred dollars a week. He's probably a low-level functionary in an embassy, and the money helps. Then I'll start asking him questions about those nursery rhymes, and that money eventually changes from a hundred dollars to a thousand. Then he starts getting comfortable telling me about some borderline things—he's touching on the edge. Pretty soon I just need him to justify his own behavior in his mind—and because I'm in control, I'll give him that justification. He's comfortable now, enjoying the benefits, and liking the risk too. Risk can be a big motivator.

SPY TRAIT #6: SPIES ARE FLEXIBLE AND READY FOR ANYTHING

SAM: I remember when I was first in training. I somehow assumed that there would be some super-cool escape plan to get me out if things went sideways. I soon learned that if things go horribly wrong there are two ways out—you can talk your way out or walk your way out. We are often sent far away, sometimes to hostile countries. As you can imagine, this can be emotionally and physically draining. But it doesn't matter how exhausted we are, we always have to be prepared to make a quick decision about our own safety or the success of the actual mission. While we have really excellent training, there are some situations you just can't prepare for—and you have to be ready to face unexpected things that require split-second decision making. And there are many times that "talking your way out" or "walking your way out" are the only options. I might try to manipulate what's happening so that I can get out of a complicated situation, or sometimes I have no choice but to immediately get off the X any way I can. There's usually no time, or no opportunity, to discuss options with anyone else. A spy must decide his best course of action and execute immediately, and often alone. I also have to be ready to adapt to any culture. This can be hard for me because I really stick out in many countries. But it doesn't matter, I have to be ready to adapt to and survive in any culture of any place that I'm sent.

THE MOSCOW RULES

ALEX often describes the craft as "requiring common sense on steroids." The Moscow Rules are a great example of this. These rules were developed over many years and instructed U.S. intelligence officers in the Soviet Union on how to engage with the KGB. The story goes that these rules were never even written down. They evolved over time, and everyone understood that following the rules to the letter was required if you wanted to survive on the streets of Moscow, which was considered the most difficult environment to operate in. The original list contained forty rules, but it's the ten following rules that MATTER MOST:

1. Assume nothing.
2. Never go against your gut.
3. Everyone is potentially under opposition control.
4. Don't look back; you are never completely alone.
5. Go with the flow, blend in.
6. Vary your pattern and stay within your cover.
7. Lull them into a sense of complacency.
8. Don't harass the opposition.
9. Pick the time and place for action.
10. Keep your options open.

REAL SPIES IN ACTION

Now that you have a better sense of what intelligence officers do to recruit spies in foreign territories in the name of keeping America safe . . . you're going to see them in action. The following stories will take us all over the world, where anything can happen. These individuals are some of the best in their field, and they use tradecraft to get the job done right. A spy never knows what skills an operation might require, and he has to be ready to use everything in his arsenal and there's no room for error. That means always being ready to conduct a five-hour surveillance detection route, use secret signals to communicate with a recruit, elicit information from someone, and be ready to answer questions while undercover if you have to. As you're about to see, these people will do whatever it takes to stay alive.

CHAPTER TWO

WHEN ONE MISSION BECOMES TWO

Using Cover Stops, Hunker-Down Sites, and Secret Caches to Spy on a Terrorist Cell

THE REQUIREMENT: Collect every electronic signal emanating from the "target site." Using these collected communications samples, engineers will determine what kind of signals were being used. Once exposed, the communications will be decrypted and translated to determine the nature of an imminent terrorist threat to the United States.

PARTICIPANTS: C/O and NARRATOR Benjamin Morris, hereafter referred to as alias SAM.

C/O Christopher Davis, hereafter referred to as alias MAX.

At first glance, I thought the requirement seemed simple enough. There was strong intelligence suggesting that the government of a country in southern Asia was funding a terrorist cell, and that an attack against America was in the works. The plan was to insert me, along with my partner MAX, into the country as two businessmen looking to "expand into the area." We would be set up in an apartment strategically located close to the terrorist cell so that we could capture all communications coming and going from the cell for further analysis. But I had been around the block enough times to know that I wasn't getting the entire story.

THE REAL STORY

Years on the job taught me that there's usually an important backstory that has to be carefully dissected, and my problem-solving skills really come into play during these early stages of the assignment.

The requirement, and what clandestine operations officers (agents who are running undercover operations) are meant to do with a "hard target," comes with a lot of information. There are tasking numbers, costing allocations, jurisdictions, authorities, approvals, and prior approvals from national command authorities and even from Congress and ambassadors. But buried within all that information is the contact info for the analyst. And that's the person I always want to see. The analyst is at the heart of the issue—they're the ones who know firsthand why the United States needs a clandestine operation to deal with a specific threat. My job isn't easy, and all I have to go on is the information from the analyst. I'm the one who has to actually carry out the deed. I have to slip into a foreign country, blend in, gain access to places no one else has been able to get to, then get out without leaving a trace.

THINK LIKE A SPY:
RESEARCH GIVES YOU AN EDGE

Spies know that doing deep research puts you one step ahead of the game. Research can be the key to success, and I believe this is true for everyone, no matter what your end goal. I can say that almost all of my success in life, whether with the Agency or now in the private sector, has come from doing the deep research and hard work that most people will never do. The fact is, deep research will not only save a case officer's life, but it will save your own life in the regular world. This is why I put together a free special report at www.SurviveLikeaSpy.com that shows you how to do deep research like a CIA operative to help you get ahead in all areas of your life.

ONE MISSION BECOMES TWO

I was right—there was definitely more to the story. MAX and I learned something very interesting from our meeting with the analyst. We were being sent to southern Asia to capture the communications between a foreign government and a terrorist cell, but it turned out that the U.S. government had their eyes on a bigger prize. The best target, the one that would provide the most information, happened to be a heavily guarded foreign government building smack-dab in the middle of the city center—*very risky*. The analysts knew that the foreign government was using a special office in the highly protected building to transmit clandestine instructions using radio-frequency disguising and multilevel encryption to the headquarters of the terrorist cell. If we could get a shot of the building showing exactly where the secret antenna was pointed, the United States would be able to intercept the communications to the terrorist cell. This was the surest way to prevent an attack on America.

But the State Department was worried about major damage to diplomatic and foreign relations if something went wrong and we got caught. So that idea was shut down and a new target was selected.

"Too risky" just weren't words guys like us understood—a big risk just made everything more interesting. We had gone undercover countless times, posing as everything from salesmen to researchers. We were both ex-military, and we worked well together. I had been in the Air Force and MAX had been in the Navy. This meant we both really understood the importance of national security beyond the confines of the job. However, this also tended to get us into trouble. One quick glance at MAX, and I knew we were thinking the same thing. We would get the surveillance as directed in the requirement, but we were going to do all we could to capture the intelligence from that original target too—we were going to do our best to find that secret antenna on that government building. The challenge became how we could get to the original target without getting caught, killed, or locked away in a foreign prison for life. Not to mention losing our jobs for not following orders. We didn't know how we were going to do it, but we were determined to give it a try. And that's how one mission became two.

THE SAFE SITE

If I'm running for my life during a clandestine mission, I need to know exactly where I'm going at all times, and I know I'll never have a second to look at the GPS on a smartphone either (if I actually have a phone). If I'm being chased, I don't want to turn a corner and find there's a fence right in front of me. Something that simple and dumb could result in my getting killed or captured and tortured in a foreign prison. That's why spies pay a visit to the Defense Mapping Agency (DMA) during the crucial planning stages of the op. The DMA has actual, physical maps of nearly every location on the globe. Every detail matters, and guys like us need to know the absolute fastest way to get to and from the location where we're hiding out. We need to be familiar with every street, power grid, and ditch. Comparative elevation and changes in local traffic throughout the day are important too. We take all the detailed information about streets and topography and compare them to street photos taken from satellites and recon flights. If there's an obstacle—like a construction site or even a pile of dirt—we aren't going to be surprised by it.

THINK LIKE A SPY: KNOW THE AREA

Always make it a point to be familiar with your surroundings—at work, at home, at school, and wherever you're traveling. If there's ever a terrorist attack or natural disaster, you need to know the backstreets, and know which streets to avoid. You'll need to have an idea of where you can hunker down to stay safe or seek shelter. Being familiar with your surroundings can also help you notice when something is off—signaling that you need to be aware of potential danger. Also, don't forget to have a physical map of your local area in your home and car in case you have to evacuate and GPS is down and won't be able to tell you the back roads.

All of this information helped us figure out the perfect location to carry out the mission. We had our eyes on a fifth-floor apartment on the west side of the building that had a clear view of our target. This location also put us close to a discreet path, so that we could bring in our special-ops gear right under the noses of the local population without anyone suspecting a thing. We would also have a few places along the ingress/egress route to stash some special-ops items, because a spy never knows when they're going to have to "sterilize a path," meaning purposely remove anything (all materials and devices used in the op) that would identify the United States' involvement in a covert operation in or out of the safe house.

But things don't always go as planned, and spies don't always get what we want. The in-country undercover case officer tried to lease the apartment. But guess what? It was already rented and the case officer couldn't buy out the lease. The only option was for the case officer to get an apartment as close to that one as possible.

BEAT IT TO FIT, AND PAINT IT TO MATCH

There's a motto written on the board right outside of my DO's (directorate of operations') door. "Beat it to fit, and paint it to match." That pretty much describes what really goes on in the world of espionage. Spying is much messier and less precise than you might expect. I can't depend on order, precision, reliability, or a dependable game plan. I am constantly faced with situations that don't go as expected, and if I want to succeed, the only thing to do is "beat it to fit and paint it to match." That is, I'll do the best I can with whatever I've got. Not a bad bit of life advice either.

The second apartment created one big problem for us. That first apartment was so ideally located that we were just going to use our clandestine espionage equipment from inside the apartment, shielded by nothing but a sheer pair of curtains. Not exactly high-level espionage tactics. But now we had to figure out how to do this without exposing ourselves. Luckily MAX knew exactly where to go to solve this problem.

THE RIGHT CONCEALED GEAR:
THE REAL WORLD OF Q

Throughout history, spies have used some fascinating gadgets. The British Special Forces created a pipe designed to kill by shooting out a small projectile at close range. The Romanian Intelligence Service designed a bugging device that fit into the heel of a shoe, and the CIA even made a pair of eyeglasses dipped in cyanide. If an officer opted for death over being subjected to torture, all he had to do was lick the stems of his glasses, and game over. Sometimes it's a particular challenge that dictates the kind of gear a spy needs, and in this case we needed something to help us collect information from a less-than-perfect location without arousing any suspicion.

The Fabrication Center could be described as "the real world of Q." It houses a fascinating collection of experts—seamstresses, carpenters, machine shop and metal workers, and even furniture makers. These experts can quickly create items that can help a spy reach their ultimate goal . . . from miniature fountain-pen cameras to fake passports so convincing they'll get through customs. Or, as was the case for this mission, the world's craziest patio umbrella.

After studying various photographs of the area, MAX noticed it was very common for people to have a patio umbrella on their terrace or balcony. MAX decided that a patio umbrella would be the perfect place to secretly house antennae for wide-band radio-wave collections. In addition to looking similar to everyone else's umbrellas, this one would contain a battery that could be recharged using the local power supply and have a storage device in the mast that could hold all of the material we collected. It would need to come apart, since we didn't want to draw attention to ourselves by walking around carrying a giant umbrella. We also had to consider scenarios where things could go wrong. What if it's windy and the umbrella goes over the balcony? What if it rains and the electrical components get wet? Will it fit on the balcony? What would happen if there was a power surge? Everything was thought through, and after three short days we had this critical piece of "concealment gear" in our hands and were ready for the next phase of the mission.

THE COVER

DATE, TIME, & PLACE: September 25, 19XX, 12:30 p.m., XXX XXXXXX Street, Apt. X XXXXX, XXXXX XXXXX.

Unfortunately, MAX became very ill with the stomach flu on our long flight over to Southeast Asia. MAX was so sick that he couldn't even leave the apartment we rented and I had to bring him all of his meals and medicine for an entire week. This meant I was going out frequently to get food, and visiting the pharmacist to get him medicine, and popping into other stores for things like blankets and pillows. Every time I went into a shop, I chatted up the proprietor. I made sure to talk about my "sick business partner" and how we had come to the area hoping to "expand our business." The local business owners were helpful, and I was sure to praise them for their role in helping my buddy feel better. I also asked lots of questions about the area, and learned about local things I could do while my "business partner" recovered.

If you're suspecting that MAX wasn't really sick, you're right. This was all part of a cover, and the "illness" was a crucial part of our preparations. The sick-colleague story meant I had a reason to go back and forth from the apartment, and this served several purposes. The repetitive trips allowed me to transport many non-alerting items. Who's going to be concerned about some guy carrying a couple of grocery bags? I could also see that the route I was taking was mainly used by local children, with some occasional foot traffic from other people going to shops. This was great news, because it meant it was an ideal pedestrian pathway for a "dead drop"—a standard move in tradecraft. A dead drop is a method of exchanging information between a case officer and an agent. An item (notes, tool, codebook) is inserted into a concealment device, and then dropped in a predetermined place for the other person to later retrieve.

While I was supposedly carrying around bags of snacks and medicine, I was actually picking up strategically placed communication devices for the umbrella, and some other spy equipment that was crucial to the mission. This ruse went on for a few days, and allowed me time to collect and transport all of the espionage gear into the "safe site" and set up operations properly. Once they were set up, we could move around with relative ease as two businessmen, and start the important work of capturing the intelligence that could prevent a devastating terrorist attack on Americans.

When all of our equipment was set up, we began casing the site in the tasking order. Everyone bought the sick businessman story, and no one would have guessed that the umbrella was being used to listen in on a terrorist cell. While I was out "running errands," MAX was sitting under the umbrella "recovering" with a cup of tea using our clandestine radio receiver in the umbrella to collect every message the target sent, 24/7. We were close to fulfilling our mission, and were supposed to wrap everything up in the next couple of days. But neither of us could stop thinking about that other target . . . the one the government had deemed too risky. Time was running out, and we still didn't have a plan for capturing the shot.

THE TRAFFIC JAM AND THE UNEXPECTED SURPRISE

DATE & TIME: October 8, 19XX, 3:30 p.m.

I was not happy when the taxi driver told me there had been an accident and he was taking a detour. I was exhausted from being up nights watching the official target, and the city was sweltering hot and smelled like garbage. Worst of all, I still had no idea how to capture a photo of the original target. Time was ticking, and we were leaving in a couple of days. I was about to tell the driver to just let me out, when he told me he was taking Avenue X, a street that wasn't used much by local traffic. I could barely believe what I was hearing . . . did the driver just say he was going down the exact road where the secret government building was located? Could this actually be the opportunity to get the shot? My palms started to sweat as the taxi went down the street, slowly but surely getting closer to the secret building. I was frantically thinking about the best way to exploit this opportunity. I had to work fast and carefully. Like any good spy, I always have a camera ready, and we were getting close enough that I could snap a picture. But how could I do it without getting caught?

THINK LIKE A SPY: TAKE ADVANTAGE OF OPPORTUNITIES

Good spies can think and adapt quickly to any situation. If you want to be a good spy, you need to think on your feet. Just like successful businessmen can take advantage of an unexpected opportunity, a good spy is ready to look at any situation and figure out how to use it to their advantage. Bottom line: If you're not resourceful, you'll never be a good spy. And, in your own life, if you're not resourceful it's going to be much tougher to survive a crisis such as a blackout, economic collapse, or natural disaster.

The taxi stopped. There was total gridlock. Obviously my taxi driver wasn't the only one who thought to take this route. I was careful not to show my excitement. To the driver, I seemed like any tired tourist, annoyed by the heat and the delay. The taxi kept crawling for what felt like ages, until suddenly there it was . . . the target I was desperate to capture. My heart sank a bit when I saw the shot was being blocked. All that stood between me and the photo was a hideous fountain—but I wasn't going to let that stop me from possibly taking down a terrorist cell.

I suddenly announced to the driver, "Wow! That is a really beautiful fountain! Can you take a picture of me in front of it?" I sensed the driver was really hesitant . . . it was obvious the building was heavily guarded. Much to my relief, the driver agreed. I hopped out, praying under my breath that the shot would include the secret antenna. As soon as the shot was taken, armed guards appeared out of nowhere and started shouting. The driver and I hurried back into the cab and were on our way. I didn't yet know if I got the shot, but I knew this was the best possible chance I was going to get, and I was anxious to get back to the safe site to secure the picture.

FAVORITE SPY TOOL: SPY FILM

I have a huge weathertight storage container I keep in the garage. At first glance it seems to be full of innocuous and uninteresting photographs taken from around the world. But each photo is actually a reminder of a particular mission I was on in each country. Spies use ordinary cameras that take extraordinary film. Since most of the pictures we take are incriminating, the film is a special variety that can be developed only by the CIA. If I'm ever caught and my camera is taken, the film contains nothing that could get me killed or land me in jail for the rest of my life.

WAS I BEING FOLLOWED?

My heart was pounding right through my chest. I was thrilled that I might have gotten the shot, but there was a bigger problem that needed to be handled immediately. If I had picked up plain-clothed security detail at the facility, I could lead them right back to the safe site, where MAX was busy operating the most high-level espionage gear on the planet. No cover story, however compelling, would let either of us walk away from that scenario. If we were caught now, not only would the hostile foreign government capture cutting-edge technology, they'd know we were aware that their government was involved in terror plots. If this happened, things would end very badly for us. However, if I was stopped, all they'd get was my pitiful cover story about wanting to photograph a fountain and a camera containing a role of worthless film. I had to make absolute sure I wasn't under surveillance before heading back to the safe site.

THE HIDING PLACE

Pilots need to be aware of emergency landing sites—big empty fields, or water in a worst-case-scenario situation. It's the same for spies. If I ever suspect I'm under surveillance, I have to figure it out for sure. In this case, I couldn't risk being followed back to the safe site. This meant I had to keep working my cover. I needed to be as slow and non-alerting in my behavior as possible, just popping into different "cover stops," various shops and cafés, looking like a tourist—hopefully boring anyone who had me under surveillance into a state of disinterest.

After visiting my preplanned cover stops, I still wasn't completely sure I was out of the woods. I headed toward my "hunker-down site," a spot I had carefully chosen soon after arriving in Asia. This was a place where I could wait—for hours, or sometimes days—to make sure I wasn't being followed. While I was out picking up stuff for my sick colleague, I had noted that some homeless people congregated under a bridge. Not the most comfortable spot to kill time, but it was the perfect hunker-down site. To ensure I'd be welcome, I had dropped off some extra food for the people under the bridge when I was initially out creating my cover. After a few long hours under that bridge, I was confident I hadn't been followed and headed back to the safe site.

WAS IT ALL WORTH IT?

I made it back to the safe site without being apprehended—a good sign, but I didn't feel out of the woods yet. There was a lot on the line. While my actions were all in the name of keeping America safe, taking that photograph had actually been a big risk. If we were exposed, the consequence would be catastrophic damage to U.S. national security. I couldn't help but wonder if forces were assembling outside, ready to burst in and throw us both in jail. In a foreign prison we would be subjected to unspeakable torture, or killed. After a sleepless night, we dismantled our gear and I made my way to the signal site to mark it, showing that the dead drop was loaded and could be serviced. Leaving the apartment and walking around town was also a way of maintaining normalcy—I was following the same routine I had established since first arriving in the country. If anyone was watching, they'd see me doing exactly what I'd been doing every day. Neither of us could breathe a sigh of relief until we landed at Dulles International Airport. It wasn't until we arrived back on U.S. soil that we were no longer in jeopardy of being detained by a hostile foreign government. We had made it back safely.

MISSION ACCOMPLISHED?

There's an unmarked building that looks like any generic office building. However, this place is anything but typical. It's actually a special site where spies take their gear to be inspected after an overseas op. This place is full of every imaginable gadget—radios, cameras, tools, ropes, special clothing, and night-vision goggles. The receptionist might look normal, but she's hiding an Uzi in her lap, and the janitorial staff is actually comprised of highly trained security experts wearing concealed body armor and weapons.

We were headed over to have our secret film developed, hoping it might contain the photo of the antenna. Bingo—we had nailed it. The antenna was clearly visible in the photograph. By using the exact coordinates of the building combined with information about the time and date I was there, the imagery analysts were able to determine the exact direction the antenna pointed. Mission accomplished.

SECRETS BETWEEN SPIES

After any mission, there's paperwork to be filled. We would be expected to create a detailed report about our mission. The report confirmed that we "successfully targeted and collected the entire set of tasking requirements on the official mission tasking." But the report was missing something. We never mentioned the photo of the antenna in our mission report. If we admitted that we had picked up hostile surveillance, we could have been blocked from future missions due to an "excessively hazardous operating environment."

Some secrets stay between spies. We had an "unofficial post mission debrief" with the same analyst who had told us about the secret antenna in the first place, and that conversation stayed completely off the record. It was during this unofficial meeting that we learned we could be sent on a new mission in southern Asia very soon. The next challenge? We were going to eliminate a terrorist operation while leaving no trace of American foreign intelligence or military involvement. Sometimes, buildings just blow up.

> **Sometimes, buildings just blow up.**

YOUR INNER SPY

I realize you may never end up in a scenario where you need to plan a clandestine mission—complete with safe sites, tricked-out umbrellas, and erasable film. However, there are a few tactics that MAX and SAM used that can help keep you and your family safe—especially in a situation where you need to hide temporarily from someone who's following you, or if there were a real threat against your life and you needed to be housed safely until the danger was over.

TACTIC #1: COVER STOPS AND HUNKER-DOWN SITES

Not long ago, my wife had an alarming experience while she was out shopping at Home Depot. She noticed that a man happened to be showing up in the same areas of the store where she was shopping—and he didn't seem to be picking up any items. She immediately started running an SDR (surveillance detection route), deliberately walking around to different sections of the store, and keeping an eye out for this man. Sure enough, he appeared in every aisle she went to. That's when she called me. I told her to ask the manager to walk her to her car, and reminded her to be vigilant about checking her mirrors to make sure this guy wasn't following her. The man did not follow her out of the store, and thankfully my wife was able to move on with her day safely. Please always remember, if you ever feel your life is truly in danger, call the police immediately. However, if you're in a situation where you aren't sure you're being followed, and you want to play it safe, simply run an SDR like my wife did, and then use a series of cover stops and hunker-down sites just like a real spy.

Cover Stops Can Be Anything, but They Need to Make Sense

SAM used his preplanned cover stops before heading to his hunker-down site. He had noted places that he might need to visit if he were trying to appear normal, when he suspected someone might have had him under surveillance.

A cover stop is any public place you can pop into. It can be a coffee shop, a restaurant, Walmart, or a grocery store. It's important, though, that cover stops make sense. You have to give the impression that you're going about your regular life. An ideal series of cover stops might be buying balloons at one store, a cake at another, and maybe one more stop for a present. You'll appear like you're shopping for a birthday party, but in reality you're carefully scanning the area, noting if you're being followed into each location. While grabbing a coffee at Starbucks is a good cover stop, don't arouse suspicion by going into a Dunkin' Donuts next. That's not likely to appear natural or authentic.

Waiting It Out: The Hunker-Down Site

After SAM ran his countersurveillance route by going to his cover stops, he headed to his hunker-down site. He wanted extra time to wait, to be sure that anyone following him would be long gone by the time he left. While hanging out under a bridge with homeless people worked great for SAM, it's important to note that a hunker-down site doesn't need to be quite so dramatic. Choose any public place where you can reasonably sit for several hours without arousing suspicion. A hunker-down site could be a café, a bar, or maybe a restaurant where you can appear to be engaged in normal behavior, while ultimately waiting for whoever might be following you to leave.

Where Could You Go?

I hope you are never followed or find yourself in any situation where you fear for your safety. But preplanning cover stops or hunker-down sites is easy, and it could keep you safe. Simply note various places near your home or workplace where you could go if you think you're being followed. How many cafés or bars are between your subway exit and your apartment building or the drive to your office? Where would you go to stay safe? What restaurants and shops are near your office or home? Which ones would you go to if you were concerned for your safety? Having a plan you can quickly execute in a dangerous situation can keep you from ending up in harm's way.

TACTIC #2: THE SAFE SITE

It may be hard to imagine a situation where you'll need a safe site—but they aren't just for spies. Should you ever find yourself feeling threatened by an estranged ex or a disgruntled coworker, you can set yourself up in a safe site where no one can find you. Forget the cliché of a safe site being some underground bunker stocked with food and ammo. That's Hollywood getting it wrong again. The most important thing you need to know about creating a safe site is that it's anything you need it to be. It can be an innocuous hotel room, or a simple house on a typical suburban street. Should you ever need to be housed secretly, or provide a haven for someone else, there are a few things you need to keep in mind:

► What do you want the site to do for you? Do you want to be able to move in and out undetected?

► Do you need to be able to have lights on late at night? Do you need to be someplace where this won't be thought of as suspicious?

► Is there a particular place the site needs to be close to?

► Will you be able to discreetly come and go to collect items you may need, such as food and other supplies?

TACTIC #3: THE CACHE

SAM and MAX couldn't very well have gotten off the plane in a hostile foreign country with a suitcase full of surveillance gear. That would surely have landed them in prison. Spies get loads of training in designing dead drops and signals. Thanks to lots of preparation and planning, they have established places where the local case officer could load their gear into a well-concealed cache. In addition to a great place to dead-drop secret messages, caches are one of my favorite ways to store extra supplies and ammo in case of an extreme emergency.

The Safest Cache: A Storage Facility

The most important element of a cache, for practical purposes, is that it is located away from your primary residence. Some people who take my Spy Escape & Evasion courses (www.SpySafety .com) want to keep a cache of guns and ammo in case the government takes over. I always point out that a much more likely scenario is that your house burns down and all of your guns and ammo go with it. You want your cache of extra supplies to be outside of your home, but easily accessible. Sure, you can go ahead and bury guns and ammo, supplies, and cash in a designated area, but chances are you're not going to remember the exact spot—and obviously that won't do you any good in an emergency.

I rent a closet-sized storage space at a storage facility for about $25 a month. I pay cash, so no one would ever be able to connect me to my cache of supplies. Inside I keep cash, food, water, survival gear, and, yes, guns and ammunition. Should an extreme emergency ever occur and I can't get home—or the items in my home are destroyed—I know that I have additional supplies safely stored at my secret location.

If You Decide to Bury a Cache: Do It Right

If you really want to bury a cache, the safest way to protect your items is by building a simple PVC cache. There are a few things you need to remember if you decide to cache:

1) Remember where you buried it. You can keep this information in a small fireproof safe in your home. You can store the safe in your attic in a box marked as "clothes" along with all of the other boxes up there. You'd be surprised how many people call me and tell me they can't remember where they buried their cache.

2) Consider spreading things out. Bury some items near your home, and some near your workplace.

3) Do not purchase cheap items—you want to make sure you are burying items that will work when you need them to.

4) Never bury caches in the following places: graveyards, places with high foot traffic, in the middle of a forest where there are no visible landmarks to locate the cache.

5) All items going into your cache should be inserted into a Mylar bag and the ends should be sealed with a hot iron.

6) Wear gloves when creating your cache, or wipe down surfaces with WD-40, to eliminate fingerprints.

To create the cache itself, you'll need:

► Four-inch schedule 40 PVC pipe (four inches wide and twenty-four inches long; Home Depot sells this standard size).

► Four-inch PVC cap.

► Four-inch DWV cleanout plug.

► Four-inch female adapter (to screw into the cleanout plug).

► Oatey handy pack (a combination of PVC purple primer and PVC cement).

Once assembled, simply insert the items going into your cache into the Mylar bags and seal with a hot iron. Insert items into the cache, treat the end and cap with primer, then treat with glue and seal the cache. Some important items to include are:

► Space blanket.

► Poncho.

► Waterproof matches.

► Dryer lint in a sandwich bag (for starting a fire).

► Collapsible cup to hold water.

► Fixed-blade knife (www.NOCknife.com).

► Flashlight.

► Roll of duct tape.

► Parachute cord.

► At least one twenty-dollar bill (the more, the better).

► Water purification tablets.

► Fifty rounds of ammunition.

► Barrettes, bobby pins, safety pins.

- ▶ Light stick.
- ▶ First-aid kit.
- ▶ Food.
- ▶ Disguises such as wig, glasses, and hat.

SPY ENCOUNTERS: MAX
THE CRITICAL MISSION

While planning and preparation are a crucial part of a successful operation, intelligence officers need to be ready to take action without planning too.

There was zero heads-up.

They called me at home in the middle of the night. At 0200 hours. The caller confirmed my identity with a prescribed challenge, and simply told me I was needed on-site in ten minutes and should be prepared to stay on-mission until relieved. I always have a RON (remain overnight bag) ready to go. Mine had everything I would need for travel and to sustain myself for a few days—it included passports, cash in various foreign currencies, mission-critical gear, toiletries, and just a few undergarments. I had been trained for critical mission calls, and it becomes easy to think, "Oh, this is just a training scenario." But this time it wasn't. A hostile foreign country had taken action against a U.S. target, and recon teams were needed airborne immediately.

I remember vividly how nervous and excited I was as I drove to the airfield. I ran through everything in my head over and over. I questioned myself about what I had in my bags—was it right? I went over my mission cover story, the protocols, and the procedures. I was a senior operator at that time, and I was expected to take care of myself, but also to set an example with calmness, confidence, decisiveness, and effectiveness. It was also my duty to bolster the guys with less experience and make sure nothing was overlooked. In a critical mission there is no room for oversight, error, or mistakes of any kind.

> In a critical mission there is no room for oversight, error, or mistakes of any kind.

This particular mission required that my team and I remain on active recon for thirty-six hours straight—that means no sleep, no meals, just gulps of water, and if you need to pee, you're using a bottle. That was a tough mission, and my eyes felt like they were full of sand and they burned like acid. I started to lose the high tones in my hearing—everything sounded loud, dull, and thick. It was like being in a fishbowl, and time swirled around me. I had to repeat things to myself over and over just to stay on task, and was giving myself pep talks. I even drifted off at one point while standing up. I caught myself right before I slumped to the floor. The adrenaline rush kicked in and brought me back to the reality of the moment, and I couldn't wait for it to be over. It's a long fall to go from feeling invincible to feeling like you are at the point of physically and mentally giving up.

SEE IT IN ACTION RIGHT NOW: I've created a free training video where you can get a list of gear to put in your own personal remain overnight bag (AKA bug-out bag.) You can also get a FREE tactical bag (the same one I use as my own bug-out bag) at www.FreeBagNow.com.

CHAPTER THREE

DR. X AND THE PUFFER FISH

How Secret Signals, Covert Communication, and a Five-Hour Surveillance Detection Route Saved America from a Deadly Biological Weapon

THE REQUIREMENT: Intelligence indicates the Soviet Union is developing a biological weapon capable of killing thousands using TTX, the toxin found in the puffer fish. C/O must determine how the Soviet Union is extracting the TTX in large amounts.

PARTICIPANTS: C/O Brendan Hamilton, known to subject and hereafter referred to as alias ALEX.

Takashi Ono, hereafter referred to as alias/krypto FELIX.

It was the most disturbing intelligence I had seen in years. The Soviets were developing a biological weapon more deadly than anything we had ever seen before. They had somehow managed to extract large amounts of TTX (or tetrodotoxin) from the puffer fish, and were planning to drop the toxin on major metropolitan areas using micro-encapsulation or aerosol. The death and suffering this would cause was unthinkable. TTX is two hundred times more deadly than cyanide (and just inhaling cyanide will result in a coma with seizures, followed by cardiac arrest). Minimal exposure to TTX leads to a fast but violent death. It starts with a tingling at the mouth, then quickly shifts to paralysis, and then death. Even worse, the victim is completely conscious of what's happening the entire time. If the United States was going to stop the Soviets from unleashing this horror on innocent civilians, we had to figure out how they were doing it.

THE TARGET

PERSONALIA:

NAME/KRYPTO: FELIX

AGE: 49

HT/WT: 5'5", 129 LB

HAIR: Black, shoulder-length, straight

GLASSES: NONE

PERSONALITY/DEMEANOR/ATTRIBUTES: Quiet, reserved, soft-spoken. Leading expert on neurotoxins. Spends many hours working in office. Not very social. Wears understated clothing.

NATIONALITY/CITIZENSHIP: Japanese, Japan

KNOWN LANGUAGES: Japanese, English

PROCLIVITIES: Goes out for tea daily, takes afternoon walks through a local park several times a week. Walks to and from work.

FAMILY: Wife XXXXXXXX (39), Son XX XXXX (15)

ADDRESS: XXXXX, XXXX, XXXXX, Tokyo, Japan

TELEPHONE NUMBER: XXX-XXX–XXXX

I didn't have much to go on. Intelligence indicated that a "Dr. X" in the Soviet Union played a key role in the development of this weapon. Spies can't approach a Russian directly because Russians are immediately suspicious of Americans. An American can't just develop a Russian, so I had to find someone who had *access* to Dr. X. And that's how I ended up meeting FELIX.

The Japanese do more research on TTX than anyone else. That's because the puffer fish is a delicacy in Japan, and just one improperly prepared bite of puffer fish (or fugu, as it's called) will kill. FELIX was a PhD at a small college in Tokyo who specialized in TTX, and he had just presented a paper at a conference on neurotoxins. One of my contacts reported that there was one very interesting person who attended that conference—Dr. X himself. This meant that Dr. X could be using FELIX's research to create the bioweapon, and that FELIX could be the crucial link to Dr. X. As luck would have it, FELIX was presenting at another conference in Tokyo in just a few weeks. It didn't give me much time to prepare, but this was a fertile lead and I was determined to be ready in time. There was so much at stake.

THE PREPARATION

I only had a few weeks to nail down the perfect cover. FELIX was a PhD. In Japan, PhDs are also medical doctors. These guys have had fifteen to twenty years of education, so I needed to fit in with some highly educated people. I wasn't going to try to pass myself off as a medical doctor or a professor—it would be way too easy to get caught. I decided to present myself as a researcher from an American pharmaceutical company. That way I could tell FELIX I was curious about his research for medical purposes, and chances were he'd believe me.

A bigger challenge was that I wasn't all that familiar with Tokyo, and not knowing a city can ruin an op—or even get you killed. One of the first things I do when I start to case a new city is memorize multiple routes to and from all the places I'll be going. I'll look for shortcuts and pay attention to any shop, bar, or restaurant that I could duck into in a pinch. I noticed right away that Tokyo was full of "choke points"—there were lots of alleys, narrow streets, and bridges that funneled people into a particular area. I'd have to watch out for those. If I was being followed—or worse, chased—I didn't want to find myself trapped with no place to run. The lanes and connected alleyways could be very confusing, but at the same time they also provided great hiding places.

THINK LIKE A SPY: REASSESS YOUR SURROUNDINGS

You may think you know your town like the back of your hand. The truth is, our environments change all the time, and it's easy to miss something unless you make it a point to pay attention. Something as simple as a closed road or construction site could cause a major delay if you found yourself in an emergency situation. Make a point of reassessing your surroundings on a regular basis. Always know what changes are taking place and how they impact you directly.

I also learned that Tokyo is full of these places called "snack pubs," and they're the perfect hangouts for spies. They're like a hybrid between a café, bar, and, weirdly enough, a karaoke club. Locals spend time there just eating and drinking and doing karaoke. Some "snacks," as they are called, are open all day, some only open late at night. So whether I'm meeting a recruit during the day or running an SDR in the middle of the night, there's always one I can go to. Snacks are also found in some pretty interesting places. My favorite snack was nearly impossible to find. I had to enter a building, exit out the back, and walk up three flights of stairs on the side of the building to where it was actually located. Others were visible from the street and made perfect "intrusion points." An intrusion point is a place where you can pop inside, forcing the person to follow you in if they want to know what you're doing. If they do, you've just confirmed with as much certainty as you can that you're under surveillance.

The first time I went to a snack pub I was greeted warmly by the owner, or the "mama-san." She asked me a lot of questions, and I got the feeling that was because I was new to the place. She chatted me up while cooking food and mixing someone's drink at the same time. She knew everyone who came in and out—she was clearly the eyes and ears of the place. Tradecraft says, "Never trust anyone," but that's not something I buy into. There are many times when allowing myself to trust someone has saved my life during an op. My gut told me that having this mama-san and others like her on my side could be very handy. I started hanging out at snack pubs strategically located around the city. I got to know the mama-san at each place, and always left a big tip. When I felt like I could trust her, I gave her a very expensive bottle of cognac with some specific instructions. I told her that if any-one ever comes in asking for me, she should pour him a gen-erous drink out of my bottle. I'd reward her for any information she could give me about anyone who might be looking for me. I left each snack feeling like I was in good hands.

THE INTRODUCTION

DATE, TIME, & PLACE OF CONTACT: September 13, 19XX, 5:30 p.m., XXXXXX University, Tokyo, Japan.

The day of FELIX's presentation arrived. I put on a freshly pressed suit and combed my newly cut hair. I made sure my nails looked neat and my shoes had shine. While my look was intended to impress, it wasn't gaudy. I didn't want to over-shadow anyone. My cover was ready and I'd read all of FE-LIX's academic papers carefully. It was time to make the introduction. Once the crowd started to thin out, I walked over to FELIX and introduced myself. It was clear right away that he was shy, and not totally comfortable talking to new people. I told FELIX I found his presentation interesting—and made a comment about one of the other papers he'd published. FELIX was surprised but flattered. Clearly this wasn't something he heard very often. He started to loosen up, so I carefully started to guide the conversation where I wanted it to go. I told him, "That part of your paper about TTX. That was interesting. How did you come to that conclusion?" I was sure to conceal my excitement when he told me that it was something he "learned from a Dr. X in the Soviet Union." Now I was positive

I was on the right track. The conversation was flowing—really going well now, so I dropped a dinner invite. But FELIX wasn't interested; he told me he had too much work to do. I wasn't about to let this opportunity slip through my hands, so I had to think of another way in. Then I remembered something about his papers. I told him, "Yes, I imagine you must have to work very hard. And by the way, I thought your English was excellent." I saw FELIX wince slightly, and it was obvious I'd hit a nerve. The truth was, FELIX's writing in English was actually awkward and flawed. FELIX told me, "I am always struggling to write in English. It takes up a lot of my time." Now I knew I had him. "Oh, well, I'd be honored to help you with that. How about I come by your office tomorrow?" This offer was much more appealing to FELIX than dinner, and he readily agreed. Now I had my first meet set up, and I already knew about one of FELIX's vulnerabilities. English was his weakness, and this was something I was going to massage like crazy.

RAPPORT/ACCESSIBILITY/SUSCEPTIBILITY

During an encounter at a university where FELIX was giving a talk, C/O told FELIX that he was very interested in his research using TTX. FELIX admitted he worked with Target/Dr.X on this research. Subject declined offer to go out for dinner, but agreed to a meeting the next day. C/O will meet with FELIX under auspices of helping him with his English. FELIX is quiet, well mannered, friendly, but somewhat shy—but becomes more animated when talking about his work. He seems concerned about his ability to write academic papers well in English. He enjoys conversation about his work, and responds well to any praise about his research.

THINK LIKE A SPY: BE READY FOR PLAN B

Spies are always prepared to seize an opportunity when it arises. ALEX knew he was on to something with FELIX, and he wasn't going to let a chance to set up a meeting with him slip through his fingers just because the guy didn't want to have dinner. When the most obvious way to get a meeting didn't work, he immediately switched to a plan B. Thinking on the fly is something spies need to be comfortable doing. ALEX ultimately got the meeting, because he quickly switched gears and tried another approach.

ARE WE BEING WATCHED?

Over the next few months I met with FELIX regularly at his office or at a local café. We were getting along well and really developing a good rapport. FELIX was happy because he was getting help with his English. Of course, these meetings also provided me with a perfect opportunity to ask questions about his work, and eventually I got some highly valuable intelligence. I learned that puffer fish excrete a large amount of TTX if you electrocute them. I continued to develop FELIX, and eventually he was "witting." A witting spy is knowingly accepting compensation for the information he's giving to his agent, and he's aware that he's actually spying for the U.S. government. I started off giving him a "consulting fee" for small bits of information. Then, as that information became more important, the fees got bigger. While FELIX did accept money for the information he was giving me, his personal philosophy played a role too. We both agreed that it would be devastating if the Soviets were using FELIX's research to create a deadly weapon. FELIX felt he was doing humanity a great service by bringing me this information. Once FELIX was witting, I was able to brief him before his trips, and debrief him once he got back from the Soviet Union. We were both determined to get as much information about Dr. X's bioweapon as possible in order to prevent a horrifying mass casualty.

THE SIGNAL

PM ABORTED: October 21, 19XX, 1:30 p.m., XXX XXX Park, Tokyo, Japan.

He looked familiar, and when you're a spy, that's not a good thing. I stopped to buy a paper on my way to meet FELIX, and that's when I noticed him. It was the same guy I had seen on the street shortly after I left my apartment. Sure, it might have been a coincidence, but I couldn't risk "burning a source" or letting FELIX get caught. It would destroy the entire operation. If this guy was following me, I needed to know now. I left the shop and started walking down the street. I could see the guy moving behind me in the reflections of shop windows. I made another stop. This time I stopped in a store and bought some fruit. When I came back out, he was still there, right across the street.

When I started moving, he started moving. Not good.

I knew exactly what I needed to do next. I walked a few blocks into a nearby park, this guy trailing me the entire time. I sat on the fourth bench from the entrance and opened my newspaper. While I was reading my paper, I carefully pulled a thumbtack out of my coat pocket and pushed it into the side of the bench. The tack wouldn't be visible to anyone unless they were looking for it. And the only person who was going to be looking for it was FELIX. After about fifteen minutes I headed off. FELIX knew that what we were doing was very dangerous, and it was my job to protect him. We had discussed at length what to do before *every* PM (personal meeting) and what actions should be taken as a result. He knew that any deviation from the plan could be deadly—and not just for us. The lives of countless U.S. civilians would be at risk if our op failed.

Protocol prior to any personal meeting. In the event a meet is deemed dangerous by C/O, signal will be left at predetermined signal site, fourth bench from entrance in XXX XXX Park. A tack inserted into left side of bench indicates PM is aborted, FELIX must conduct SDR before heading to office or home. FELIX will not contact C/O until follow-up signal is received.

I was on really high alert after I aborted the meeting. Who was this guy who was following me? Was he KGB? I hoped FELIX saw the signal and would do an SDR just like I had taught him. I headed right to one of the snack pubs to see if the mama-san had any news for me. I sat at my favorite table—one with a perfect view of the door. When the mama-san poured my drink she said, "Would you like spare ribs for lunch today?" That was our code—it meant someone had been asking after me. FELIX and I were definitely being watched.

SPY ENCOUNTERS: ALEX
THE PRE-PM WORKOUT

Every intelligence officer prepares for PMs, or personal meetings, in a different way. When you are deep undercover during an op in a foreign country, it's crucial that you are mentally prepared to take a meeting with a recruit.

I've worked all over the world, deeply undercover. I've lived under twenty different cover stories. Operations have taken me from the dark underworld of Seoul, Korea, to battlefields in Iraq, and I've witnessed the horrors of genocide in Bosnia. Each place I'm sent has its own challenges, and it's important that I'm ready for anything. That's why I'm extra-cautious before an important meeting with a recruit or a target. I want to make sure I'm in the right mind-set, because blowing my cover is one of the worst things that could happen. As part of my preparations, no matter where I am I do some sort of intense workout before a meeting. It could be anything—running or weight lifting at a gym, depending on where I was. Or if I didn't have access to a gym I'd just do a lot of strenuous exercises like push-ups and jumping jacks to get my heart rate up. The exercise helps me relax and clears my brain so I can focus on the meeting. It might sound weird, but I also make sure I'm never really full or starving—I don't want anything, even the most minor thing, to distract me from what I'm doing. This is so important to my process that if I don't feel a hundred percent good and ready after my workout—if in my mind I'm not positive things are going to work my way—I'll cancel the meeting. It's not something I ever want to do, but it's better than messing up the meeting and putting the whole op in jeopardy.

THE FIVE-HOUR SURVEILLANCE DETECTION ROUTE

DATE, TIME, & PLACE OF CONTACT: May 05, 19XX, 4:30 p.m., XXXX XXXXXX, Tokyo, Japan.

Spies always follow a surveillance detection route after a meeting. But now I had to take it up a notch. I let a few days go by, and then I signaled FELIX to meet me at a restaurant in another part of the city. The meeting was successful, and I was relieved to know that besides being safe, FELIX was carefully following SDRs the way I taught him. After our meeting, I got ready for a really long night. I wanted to be extracautious, so I planned to spend the next five hours running a long surveillance detection route. I decided to make a museum my first stop. I walked around looking at different exhibits, paying careful attention to anyone who might be following me. So far, so good.

Next, I got on the subway. I rode for a few stops, got off, and then got back on in the other direction. The subways in Tokyo were packed, so while it was really hard to know if anyone was following me, I also knew that following me in this kind of crowd was nearly impossible. I had dinner with a female friend, and if anyone was watching, it would look like we were out on a date. After dinner, I took another subway ride, this time passing my stop on purpose. I got off, walked a long way to one of the more obscure snack pubs. I sat there for over two hours. Convinced I was in the clear, I went home and got some much-needed sleep. A spy has to be vigilant—always. I knew tomorrow I'd be running another long SDR. All it takes is one careless move to ruin an operation and get someone killed. And I wasn't going to let that happen, not with so many lives at stake.

> **All it takes is one careless move to ruin an operation and get someone killed.**

YOUR INNER SPY

Covert communication is really an art. While simplicity is key when using signals, it's something that must be practiced regularly to execute properly. Ultimately, though, these are skills anyone can master, and in addition to being fun, there's a practical side to them that can help you and your family stay safe.

TACTIC #1: COVERT COMMUNICATION—HOW TO SIGNAL SOMEONE LIKE A SPY

Chances are if you need to cancel lunch with a friend, you're just going to send her a text message. As you might imagine, sending texts, emails, or phone calls is not always an option for spies in the middle of an operation. And while there are some amazing gadgets used in espionage, sometimes the best way for spies to communicate is through simple signals like ALEX's thumbtack. No one other than FELIX or ALEX would notice it. But they knew exactly what would happen if the tack was ever there. Spies might also signal each other with colored tape or chalk markings.

- ▶ Decide on the signal. It could be tape, a tack, or a chalk marking. Anything simple that will not draw the attention of other people.

- ▶ Choose a location. It should be somewhere easily accessible to both parties. Also, make sure the signal does not interfere with the culture of the area. For example, the streets of Tokyo are cleaned frequently. If a chalk mark is left on a sidewalk, there's a good chance it will be washed away.

- ▶ Decide how often the signal site will be checked. Every Friday? Once a month? Daily? Only before prearranged meetings?

- ▶ Plan what each person will do when a signal is left. Does it indicate danger? That a dead drop is loaded? Or that you should abort the meeting?

Interpersonal Coded Communication: Create Your Own Spy Signals

While chalk markings and thumbtacks obviously aren't an efficient way for normal people to communicate, there are times when signals can be very useful and can keep you and your family safer. Developing simple signals and code words of your own is an excellent way to communicate with your family when you feel like you might be in danger.

- ▶ Decide on a code word, phrase, or signal that your family will use when you are in a public place and you feel a threat. To avoid confusion, don't use a common word, and don't choose one that is difficult to remember. Discuss in advance what action you will take if the signal is used.

- ▶ Come up with your own "spy phrase" to use with your children. If you approach them at the playground and use the phrase, they know that what you're really asking is if they're okay. It's also a good idea to have a second phrase, one that means, "Are you okay if I walk away?" That way your child has an easy way of discreetly letting you know if they need help.

TACTIC #2: PRO-LEVEL SURVEILLANCE DETECTION ROUTES

In my first book, *Spy Secrets That Can Save Your Life*, I touched on just a few of the fun elements involved in doing surveillance. Now I'm going to tell you how intelligence professionals run surveillance during an actual op. And the same rule of thumb I talked about in *Spy Secrets That Can Save Your Life* still applies here. One encounter = an accident; two times = a coincidence; three times = enemy action.

Run an SDR (Surveillance Detection Route) Like a Real Spy

It takes a lot of skill, planning, patience, and self-discipline for intelligence officers to do their job while under surveillance. But the stakes are high. Failing to evade surveillance in a hostile environment during an operation can have serious repercussions— national security could be compromised, and the lives of the agent and his source could be in jeopardy. Intelligence professionals understand that the nature of their work means that they are targets for hostile surveillance. This means running an SDR every time they take a meeting, no matter what. When they leave an establishment, there's no peeking over their shoulder, deciding all is clear, and just heading home. That kind of thinking will get you caught or killed.

The Elements of a Good SDR

- A well-designed SDR will get you to a meeting on time without being followed and without alerting anyone who might be watching or waiting for you to make a move.

- A good SDR is designed in advance, taking into account any obstacles that might be encountered along the way, including traffic, construction sites, one-way streets (especially if you are in a car), shortcuts, choke points, alleys, and dead-end streets.

- A spy will have memorized multiple routes to and from any meeting. They must be switched up and used randomly.

- Your SDR must give you multiple opportunities to see who might be watching you.

- Design your SDR so that you have opportunities to look behind you. This could be turning down a street, or looking in the glass of a store window to see if someone is following you. This must be done in a way that is logical and looks natural.

The Elements of Surveillance

There are many different tactics an intelligence officer can take when running an SDR. Becoming familiar with different approaches, practicing them, and being able to execute them quickly and confidently can make the difference between getting back home alive or spending the night in a foreign prison. These tactics should be woven into SDRs randomly and at different times.

Parallel Movement

On a map, note the most direct route to your meeting location. This is a logical route, and the one anyone would take under ordinary circumstances. Now that you can see the direct route, plan an SDR that parallels and crosses back and forth over the direct route. For example, in New York City, Times Square is a straight shot about ten blocks to the north of Penn Station. Any normal person would walk directly up Seventh Avenue until they reached Times Square. Parallel movement might mean walking east to Fifth Avenue, walking a few blocks north, then heading back west, snaking your way uptown until you reach your destination.

Turns

A good SDR will have several turns that enable you to look and see who is behind you. This also forces anyone who might be following you to turn the same direction, providing an opportunity for you to spot someone who is on your tail. When you incorporate a turn into an SDR, there must always be a reason for it. Pop into a store or a café. Your turns need to appear logical and purposeful. Remember that learning to execute a turn without being noticed takes practice. You can't just take a turn and look behind you without appearing conspicuous, and that's the last thing you want.

Stair-Stepping

Stair-stepping is an advanced maneuver, but it adds complexity to an SDR. Stair-stepping involves making a series of left and right turns, usually in an area where the streets are on a grid. If you plotted out this route on a map, it would look like a set of stairs. If someone is still behind you after three or four turns, it's a safe bet that you're under surveillance. This pattern will appear unusual to anyone who is watching you, so it's important that you follow it up with a logical action, like going to a bank or into a building.

Stops

Making a stop while on an SDR can be a powerful tool. ALEX did this especially well—noting various snack pubs where it wouldn't be unusual to spend quite a bit of time. As always, make it natural. Buy coffee, have a meal—whatever makes sense. Planning stops along your SDR also provides an opportunity to see who enters the location after you, and you can also note if anyone slows down to look in the window.

Channeling

Channeling is another advanced maneuver that can help you confirm if you're actually being followed. The idea is to force any surveillance to follow directly behind you. This could be well-lit tunnels, long bridges, and sections of highways that don't have exits or overpasses. If you are the target of multiple team surveillance, this will force the entire team to get into a line in what's known as a "wagon train."

Reversals

A reversal is a turn that allows you to look back to see if you're being followed. This forces anyone following you to react to you or mirror your movement. A reversal is another move that must be followed by a logical stop, or else it appears very unnatural.

You might do a reversal in a shopping mall or a department store. You'd be walking in one direction, and then you'd turn 180 degrees—ideally stepping onto an elevator or stairs. Now you're looking in the direction you just came from, and you can see what's happening without looking suspicious. Obviously to pull this off the escalator or stairs need to be facing the opposite direction from which you approached.

Dry Cleaning

Dry cleaning is when you purposely enter a building with multiple exits—like a department store or a shopping mall. Surveillance is forced to move with you, because they don't have any idea what exit you will use. Once inside, you can use reversals and stair-stepping to lure them out, so you can see where they are and what they are doing. When you leave, choose a different exit from the one you came in.

SPY ENCOUNTERS: BRYAN
COMMUNICATING TO AGENTS VIA SECRET SIGNALS

I think there's a preconceived notion that spies are trained to do amazing physical things—but that being a spy doesn't take any imagination. I have found that being creative is incredibly helpful—especially when communicating with an agent. I remember training an agent to watch for signals via an ordinary-looking radio I had him keep in the basement. It looked just like any normal radio that someone might have in his basement to listen to while working on projects. The difference was that I could drive by his house in my car, flip a switch, and a small but barely noticeable light would come on. My agent knew exactly what this meant. It meant he was supposed to go out for an evening walk through town at a predetermined time. That radio system worked like a charm.

I've also seen some signalizing that is incredibly creative. One woman worked with an agent at a large office building. The environment was such that it would have been considered very inappropriate for this woman to be speaking to her agent at work. Her system for signaling her agent was genius. She found a very distinctive scent, and her agent was trained to watch out for that scent. The agent was instructed to head to a certain stairwell or elevator at predetermined times. If she needed to meet with him, she'd pass through the area, wearing the scent so that he would pick it up during his next visit to the stairwell or elevator. That is a signal that other people just wouldn't pick up. Salt is another one. I once trained an agent—also in a building—to pay attention to the feel of salt under his shoe. He knew to visit the men's room at predetermined times, and to carefully pay attention to the feel beneath his shoes as he entered the bathroom. If a meeting was required, salt would be present on the floor, and he'd feel the grit of the salt beneath his feet.

There are countless ways to signal a person. It's all about what works best for you and your agent and the kind of environment you're in. Other than that, you can get as creative as you want.

CHAPTER FOUR

GATHERING INTELLIGENCE IN A WAR ZONE

Surviving Bombings and Brutality During a Civil War in El Salvador

THE REQUIREMENT: Collect information that will be of value to military personnel. Brief military personnel in Central America on a regular basis so that informed decisions can be made and targets can be designated.

PARTICIPANTS: Peter Kaplan, hereafter referred to as alias PAUL.

Sebastian Mercado, hereafter referred to as alias/krypto ANGEL.

The flight over was long and hellish. Even on a 747, it took forever. I was never sent on a direct route, and we made a couple of stops that were very out-of-the-way. To make matters worse, I was headed to a region where malaria was a big risk, and the medicine was lousy on the gut. By the time I got to Central America, I was wiped. But there was no time to rest up. A really vicious war was going on, and there had recently been five or six brutal battles. My job was to collect information that could help our people make the right decisions. It was basic gathering of tactical intelligence—getting HUMINT to the appropriate personnel so that they had up-to-date information to work with each day. I'm glad to say I was able to get helpful information to the military personnel on a regular basis, even though some really crazy things happened throughout the course of the operation.

My official rep was ANGEL. ANGEL was a Puerto Rican Air Force officer and we'd be working closely together. He had mastered the local dialect, knew his way around—and looked like the meanest guy you'd ever want to encounter. He had grown a Fu Manchu–style mustache, had very long hair, and made no attempt whatsoever to hide the pistol that he kept in his front belt. His first order of business was to get me to the safe house located in a protected compound. On the way over, ANGEL told me a story that chilled my blood and made me think that, while I had done this kind of work many times before, it was going to be harder and more dangerous this time around.

BRUTALITY IN THE EXTREME

ANGEL explained that the guerrillas were ruthless. They hid in the mountains during the day and came out at night. A farmer had recently suffered terribly at the hands of the guerrillas. The farmer was a wealthy landowner running a prosperous farm and had lots of land and a spacious home. One day a battalion of troops arrived and informed the farmer that they needed to camp on the farm, and they would be staying on the property for a couple of days. The farmer wasn't given any choice—this kind of duty was simply expected of him, so of course he went along with it. The troops camped out, and the farmer and his family

went about their business. After the troops left, a group of guerrillas arrived and did something unthinkable. They rounded up
the farmer, his wife, and their six children, and shot the children
one by one right in front of their parents. The farmer and his wife
were told to "let that be a lesson to you for helping the government." This is the kind of environment I was headed into—one
where brutality ruled. I would need to be prepared for anything,
since the guerrillas were capable of doing *anything*. Fortunately,
I didn't suffer anything as terrible as the farmer, but I did face a
number of situations that had me fearing for my life.

ATTACKED AT THE SAFE HOUSE

DATE, TIME, & PLACE: November 25, 19XX, 9:09 p.m.,
XXXX XXXX XXXXXXX, San Salvador, El Salvador.

ANGEL, myself, and a few others had been working very long
hours to get intelligence to the right people, including a U.S.
general. We were successfully providing up-to-date information every morning. One night we decided to give ourselves a
bit of a treat. We were all staying at a safe house located inside
a protected compound. It turns out that one of the guys managed to get a satellite TV linked up at his place, and he mentioned that a big boxing match was airing that night. We
decided to get some beer and all agreed to meet at his place to
watch. Since it's a safe house in a protected compound, it was
obviously very important that we keep our location under
wraps, and we were always very careful to make sure we
weren't being followed. That night was no different. ANGEL
and I carefully followed an SDR before entering the compound.

Beers were passed around and we all settled in front of the small TV to enjoy a quiet and relaxing evening watching the fight. It turns out our evening wasn't going to be relaxing at all. The fight had barely started when the apartment was rocked by a huge blast. The entire place shook. It felt and sounded like a bomb. I could literally smell the explosion coming toward us. I immediately dove to the floor, taking a lamp and a table down with me. We had no idea what was actually happening, but it was safe to assume that we had been followed into the compound, and that guerrillas had blasted their way in through the front gate. We were all trained to move immediately, but there was only one exit—and it was facing where the sound of the blast had come from. Using that door could mean running directly into the danger. There was nowhere to go, and the guerrillas could bust in at any minute.

THINK LIKE A SPY: ALWAYS NOTE EXITS AND ALTERNATIVE EXITS

Whenever a spy sits down in a restaurant, coffee shop, or movie theater, I guarantee you the first thing he's going to do is note the exits. He'll also likely sit in a position that enables him to see an entrance/exit, so he can pay attention to everyone who's coming in. A spy is going to look for the closest exit, but he'll also be sure to locate any other means of escape in case something happens. This could mean using an exit that is on the other side of a restaurant kitchen, or even a window. Get in the habit of noticing exit points when you go out in public. It could save your life someday.

We had to prepare to defend ourselves immediately. We moved as much furniture as we could to barricade the door and had our weapons ready to go. There was nothing else we could do but sit silently, weapons waiting, keeping down low and as quiet as possible. We barely moved for the next hour. The guerrillas hadn't busted in, and eventually we had to assume it was safe to go outside. We were incredibly fortunate. That blast wasn't meant for us—the guerrillas hadn't found our safe house after all. They had come down from the mountains at night just to blow up some telephone poles. It was an act of economic sabotage, but it showed me that in war-torn Central America you couldn't let your guard down for a single second.

WHEN VIOLATING CURFEW NEARLY GOT US KILLED

DATE, TIME, & PLACE: April 4, 19XX, 11:30 p.m., San Salvador, El Salvador.

I saw things in Central America that I'm glad to say I've never seen again. There was so much violence in the capital that the embassy in El Salvador established a curfew. There wasn't supposed to be anyone on the street after dark, and violating this curfew could mean getting yourself killed. It wasn't un-common for guerrillas on motorcycles to terrorize innocent people. Just stopping a car at a stop sign could be deadly. Guerrillas would work in teams of two. They'd pull up next to a stopped car and unload an entire magazine—killing every-one inside. Many people lost their lives in this random, sense-less way.

As in any war zone, San Salvador had areas that were hot-beds of violence, and these places were to be avoided at all costs. The university was an example of a no-go area, as it was a place where propaganda was published and distributed. At the time, a naval attaché had recently shown some very poor judgment by dating a university student—and it cost him his life. One day she asked him to pick her up. It turns out she had fingered him to the bad guys and he was murdered in the middle of the university café. And if all that wasn't bad enough, unemployment was rampant, and there were about fifty thou-sand guerrillas and government troops roaming around the city. We also knew that the government could commandeer your vehicle if they felt like it. You could be out at night in your car, told to get out, and then be left standing alone on the street with nothing. Needless to say, we took the curfew seriously and were reluctant to go out at night unless we really had to.

THINK LIKE A SPY: A SPY'S REAL NO-GO AREA?

You can lose your life if you practice bad tradecraft—especially in a no-go area.

While that's obviously a much more dramatic situa-tion than anything you'll ever face, and you likely won't have to avoid any no-go areas, any spy will tell you to stay away from big crowds. They're dangerous. And yes, for some people that might mean choosing to avoid some ex-citing activities such as sporting events, concerts, or parades—anything that draws a large number of people into the same space. I understand that many people don't want to miss out on activities they enjoy because of fear. If you're going to be in a big crowd, it's critical that you continue to practice good situational awareness. You need to notice what's going on around you, be on the lookout for anyone who doesn't fit in or is acting strangely, and be ready to act accordingly.

One night in April, ANGEL and I were working really late. It was after eleven p.m. and we still hadn't had any dinner. ANGEL said he was starving, and that he knew McDonald's would still be open. I was wearing a pistol in a shoulder holster, and I threw a light jacket on over it, since it was still a bit cool. We got in the car, drove carefully to the restaurant, and arrived without incident. ANGEL went in to get the food, and I waited for him in the car. Violence and crime had gotten so bad that it wasn't uncommon to see heavily armed security guards all over the place. Out of the shadows, I saw a security guard carrying a massive automatic shotgun and he was walking right toward me. He directly approached the car and pointed the gun right in my face.

I couldn't believe it. I'd survived in different war zones all over the world, but I was going to die in a McDonald's parking lot—shot by an amateur security guard with an incredibly powerful weapon. I could see right away that he was very agitated. I was still smoking then, and the only thing I could think to do was to offer him a cigarette. He nodded yes, and I handed him the cigarette and lit it for him, careful not to let my hands shake. I could see that he was starting to relax while he smoked. Just then ANGEL arrived. They exchanged a few words in Spanish, and they were suddenly both laughing.

ANGEL explained that this guy just wanted to see my gun. I pulled my coat back and showed him my pistol. He gave me a smile, and we headed off, and once again I was just thankful to have gotten through another day alive.

THINK LIKE A SPY: DIFFUSE A DIFFICULT SITUATION

Any good spy will tell you that you never want to get in a confrontation, especially a physical one, unless you have to. Quick thinking was used to take this guy's level of agitation down with an offer of a cigarette, and it worked. If PAUL had reached for his gun, it's entirely possible the security guard would have shot him with his much more powerful weapon. Never escalate a situation—always attempt to diffuse it. (However, if you can't diffuse a situation and you are forced to defend yourself, you need to know quick and devastating self-defense moves that can get you out of any situation. Check out www.SpyCombatives.com for what intelligence officers use.)

> Never escalate a situation—always attempt to diffuse it.

YOUR INNER SPY

War-torn countries are incredibly dangerous places. They are volatile, and there's a high risk of getting hit by a bullet or being caught in an explosion. Many CIA officers spend time in war zones, and I hope this is something you'll never have to experience. But as you know, we are living in an unpredictable time, and many of us worry about terrorist attacks, or attacks by a "lone wolf." What would you do if you heard an explosion? What would you do if you were out with your family and a bomb went off? How would you handle a situation where you were faced with a threatening individual who was determined to do you harm?

TACTIC #1: WHAT TO DO IN AN EXPLOSION

Everyone's Greatest Fear: Improvised Explosive Devices

It's every American's greatest fear. You're out and about, maybe going shopping at the mall or just walking down a city street on your way to dinner, when suddenly the ground shakes violently beneath your feet. The sound is deafening, and before you can comprehend what is going on you're thrown several feet into the air. Chaos ensues—people are hurt, bleeding, screaming, shards of glass and metal are all around you. A bomb has gone off. Americans watched in horror as bombs went off just twelve seconds apart near the finish line of the Boston Marathon in 2013. More recently, in 2016, we saw a bomb go off on a New York City street, terrorizing residents who were going about everyday activities such as coming home from the grocery store or walking their dogs.

Improvised explosive devices (IEDs) are a major concern in the age of terrorism. While IEDs are often deadly, you can arm yourself with some basic knowledge that could help you survive a bombing. Using a combination of situational awareness, common sense, and practicing the "zero, five, and twenty-five" technique can save your life.

When the Blast Hits: The Two Actions That Can Save Your Life

Stay Low or Flat on the Ground

When the blast occurs, the first and most important thing you need to do is hit the ground and stay as low as possible. You should grab on to anything you can so that you aren't tossed around. If you are in a building, try to crawl under a table or any heavy object that can protect you from falling debris. Stay away from windows, big mirrors, electrical equipment, or unstable, tall furniture such as bookcases that can fall on you. Wherever you end up, it's crucial you remain low—completely flat on the ground if possible. The bomb may have been designed to toss shrapnel, which can be deadly. The debris is most likely going to hit people near the torso and head. Staying low could help save you from dying or being seriously injured from shrapnel.

Take Slow, Shallow Breaths

During a traumatic event like this, it's normal to take big deep breaths or gasp for air—but when a bomb hits, taking slow and small breaths through your mouth can save your life. What most people don't know is that during an explosion, dying from internal bleeding in the lungs is also a big concern. Death from "blast lung" can occur even if there isn't an injury to the chest. The pressure from the blast can be so strong that it actually can cause the lungs to blow up like a balloon, resulting in serious internal injuries. In Israel, where terrorist attacks are unfortunately common, some hospitals have reported that more than half of the serious injuries from an explosion occur this way.

You Survived the Initial Blast. Now What?

Again, it sounds impossible to do, but you need to stay calm so that your brain can process what's happening and you can make good decisions. It's human nature to freeze—but in many cases, doing nothing and being in a state of shock can get you killed. But equally important, while it's crucial that you react, running away isn't necessarily the right thing to do. You have to carefully observe your immediate surroundings first.

If You Are Inside

You are at work or maybe in a store shopping when a bomb goes off. You took temporary shelter under a large table or desk. What's your next move?

You'll want to exit the building after waiting about a minute to ensure you won't be hit by any falling debris. You'll need to move as quickly as possible. If police or the fire department has arrived to help, follow their orders. If not, carefully make your way through any debris to an exit. But don't use an elevator. It might be tempting to use your cell phone to call for help, but don't. It's possible that an electrical signal or a spark from an electronic device could trigger another explosion. Once you are out of the building, move away from it as quickly as possible.

If You Are Out in Public: Zero, Five, and Twenty-Five

You're walking down the street on your way home from work or maybe you're at a sporting event or an outdoor concert when the explosion occurs. You survive the initial blast and are lying flat on the ground. What should you do next?

In *Spy Secrets That Can Save Your Life* I talked about "getting off the X"—in other words, doing whatever you need to do to get out of harm's way immediately. While you want to get out of the way during an explosion, you must proceed very carefully before running away. The rule of thumb with an explosion is this: *if there was one bomb, there's probably more.* You don't want to run from the initial explosion site just to end up being blown up by a second bomb. It isn't unusual for terrorists to plant bombs in such a way that the first explosion will drive crowds of people from one area—only to have them all hit when the second bomb goes off. It's never safe to assume you are out of harm's way after one explosion. Expect a second one, and if you want to survive, you're going to do exactly what U.S. soldiers stationed in Iraq do.

Zero, Five, and Twenty-Five

Improvised explosive devices are the number one cause of death for U.S. troops in Iraq. In order to save lives, the Army adopted an idea from a tactic that was originally used by British forces operating in the North of Ireland. The "zero, five, and twenty-five" refer to the diameter of the circle around you from the place you are standing. The idea here is to always check your immediate surroundings before making a move. Look down toward your feet. Do you see something that could be an explosive? What about the next five feet? Slowly observe the space in the five feet around you. Does it look safe? If it does, check out a bigger distance, twenty-five feet. Are there any objects that look like they might explode? A suitcase, backpack, or even an oddly parked abandoned car? If not, carefully make your way through the debris and away from the site of the bomb.

If You Are Trapped Under Debris

People do survive explosions, even after being trapped under debris. After the September 11 tragedy, a Port Authority worker was miraculously found alive after having been buried in debris for twenty-seven hours. She was located by a trained rescue dog and pulled to safety by first responders. If you survive the blast but are buried under rubble, there are a few things you can do to increase your chances of survival and to alert authorities that you need to be rescued.

Your instincts may tell you to move around or try to climb out—but don't. You don't want to disturb debris, inhale dirt and dust, and risk getting buried further. You will increase your chances of staying alive if you remain calm, stay still, and carefully try to draw attention to yourself. If you can, cover your mouth with a part of your clothing. You want to avoid having your mouth filled with dirt or dust, inhibiting your ability to breathe. Avoid yelling if possible. Again, you don't want to end up with a mouthful of debris. If a pipe or wall is nearby, make consistent tapping noises to alert the attention of rescue workers.

TACTIC #2: THREAT ASSESSMENT—WHAT YOU NEED TO KNOW IF YOU ARE FACED WITH A THREATENING INDIVIDUAL

What happened to the farmer and his family outside San Salvador is truly horrific—and thankfully such extreme tragedies don't happen very often. Obviously, El Salvador was a very dangerous place to be during a time of war—and fortunately that's not the kind of environment we're living in. However, when

ANGEL told PAUL that story, he knew he needed to be prepared to deal with a *threat*. In that case, the threat was coming from people who were angry, living in a war-torn country, and ultimately not behaving rationally. Unstable people can be very dangerous, and it doesn't take something as drastic as civil war to cause instability. Any crisis—whether an emotional one, an illness, or a financial problem—can put people in a position where they feel unstable, overly emotional, and more likely to exhibit irrational behavior. Before I go any further, let me just say if you truly feel threatened, as always your first course of action should be to avoid the conflict, contact the police, and only use physical violence as a last resort.

A famous example of irrational behavior that most of us are familiar with is John Hinckley, Jr.'s shooting of President Ronald Reagan and several others in 1981 to impress the actress Jodie Foster. Hinckley had sent a letter to Ms. Foster explaining that what he was about to do (assassinate the President of the United States) was an expression of his love for her. That's obviously not rational. Hinckley had followed Foster to Yale University, had tried to contact her by phone, and had also written letters. After the assassination attempt, Hinckley even claimed the shooting had resulted in Foster being one of the most famous actresses in the world. That's clearly twisted logic.

So what do you do if a person in your life—a coworker, an ex, someone in your neighborhood—starts behaving in an irrational manner? What should you do if someone is threatening your safety, harassing you, or accusing you of doing something you didn't do? When dealing with upset human beings, whether in a war zone, the workplace, or even your neighborhood, it's important to remember that your decision making becomes more emotional than rational. However, there are some guidelines you can follow to be more secure.

Assessing Your Threat Level

Can Your Threat Actually Get to You?

Before you completely panic and do something drastic like change your identity or disappear off the grid (I covered this process in detail in *Spy Secrets That Can Save Your Life*, and I also explained why this is difficult to do and should only be a last resort), you need to determine your threat level. Can this person get to you? Or can you get away from them? My business partner in our corporate security firm (www.GPIagents.com) was working with a group of people who help young women escape from child traffickers. They felt threatened by the traffickers and naturally wanted to keep the girls safe—so they were hiding the girls away in the basement. When my colleague pressed them for more information about the threat, he learned that the traffickers were located five states away. He realized that while the girls were hiding in the basement, they weren't securing their perimeter properly. They weren't locking doors and gates or using a security system. In this case, he felt that it was unlikely the threat could get to the girls, so it was unnecessary to hide them away, but that they should continue practicing good safety measures, and that meant locking doors, windows, and gates, and using an alarm system to secure the premises.

Are You Being Threatened by an Individual?

If you've been subjected to irrational behavior or have been frightened or harassed, you need to determine what basic information you have about the individual in question.

- ▶ Who is this person? Do you know them? Are they a co-worker, an ex, someone who lives in your area?
- ▶ What do they do? Where do they work?

- ▶ Where are they located? Are they local or is there a good distance between you?
- ▶ What is their emotional state? Are they distraught by death, divorce, job loss, or illness? Is it possible they feel like they have nothing to lose? You must remember that people who feel like they have nothing to lose can be dangerous and may take their behavior to extremes.

After asking yourself these questions you should note a couple of things. First, if the threat is local, you'll have to be on alert (and there are tips for measures to take at the end of this chapter). If the threat is not local, do not go crazy worrying about something that probably won't happen. For example, if the individual who is threatening you lives on the other side of the country, it's unlikely that you need to worry about them arriving on your front steps. If you are still in contact with the person who is threatening you, *stop all contact with them immediately*. You should also ask family members to stop being in touch with this person. You want to document all of this information and provide it to law enforcement. In addition to answering the questions above, keep clear records of every instance when this person has been in contact with you. This includes visits, phone calls, texts, and emails. I recommend keeping a journal of events, including dates, times, and other detailed information that can help police stop your stalker.

It's also important to note that you don't have to forgive irrational behavior because someone is dealing with difficult circumstances—and you absolutely shouldn't ignore it. Unbalanced behavior should never be disregarded simply because a person is dealing with a job loss or a divorce.

Are You Being Threatened by a Group?
Sometimes it's a group or organization that is posing the threat. For example, maybe you're being targeted because you are in a

position of authority and a decision you made didn't go over well. Or maybe an organization you are connected with disagrees with your viewpoints and you find yourself being harassed. Whatever the situation, you need to determine some basic information about the specific group you're having a problem with.

- ▶ How big is the group? Is it a few local people, or a large organization with chapters nationwide?
- ▶ What is the group dynamic? Are they peaceful? Do they have a history of perpetrating violence?
- ▶ Do you have an ally in the group?
- ▶ Who is the key individual and what is their position? Is it a leader of a local branch who's bothering you? Why is this person targeting you?
- ▶ What does the organization do? Is this a motorcycle gang with a criminal history? Are their views extremist? Is it a cult? If there is a radical element, know that it is simply not possible to reason or argue with them. You will not win.
- ▶ Is it a religious or cultural institution?

You shouldn't approach the group that's bothering you if you feel you are in physical danger—again, that's a job for the police. However, if you don't feel the group poses a true threat to your life and you feel you can take a proactive approach in handling the problem, this is often an effective way of managing the situation. Just remember, opposition creates more opposition. You do not want to create more opponents—and that's exactly what will happen if you approach the group and behave in a hostile or belligerent manner. Do not visit the group in person,

Opposition creates more opposition.

threatening to do harm if they don't leave you alone. Do not antagonize the group further by posting negative comments about them on social media or other public outlets. This will only make the situation worse and possibly more dangerous for you. Instead, include the information from the questions above to the police. Keep a very detailed journal, carefully noting every instance when they have harassed or threatened you, and give this information to the police.

I'm Facing a Threat. Now What?

If you are facing an individual or group threat, you must increase your personal awareness. In *Spy Secrets That Can Save Your Life* I talked about the importance of understanding and implementing situational awareness and Cooper's color code. In this case, you'd need to increase your level of situational awareness to Orange. That means you are alert to probable danger and prepared to take action. You don't want to go to Red or action mode. Our brains cannot function in a Red state for a prolonged period of time. You need to let your brain process both fast and slow thinking, and that cannot happen in Red.

Always Remember: MORE AWARENESS = MORE DILIGENCE = MORE DETERRENCE

- ▶ Increase communication: Let your family members know what's going on. Keep them posted on your plans—let them know where you are going, how you are getting there, and when you anticipate coming back.
- ▶ Inform the police and keep an accurate record of all threats—emails, phone calls, personal attacks out in public, and threatening letters.

▶ Increase your awareness of your community and immediate surroundings. Note strangers and unfamiliar vehicles. Pay attention to any strangers who are lurking around.

▶ Listen to your children. Children are incredibly observant. If your child notes that someone in your immediate vicinity has a weapon, pay attention and get out of the area immediately.

▶ Change routines. Don't be an easy target. Drive different routes to work and leave the house at different times. Shop at a different grocery store. Always pay attention to individuals who might be following you, and never drive directly to your house if you suspect you are being followed. Remember how spies run an SDR (surveillance detection route) and how you can do the same.

▶ Take countermeasures. Always lock your doors and windows, and make sure your security system is on at all times. Use it while away *and* when you're at home.

SPY ENCOUNTERS: STEPHEN
I SURVIVED BECAUSE I LEARNED FROM THE VETERANS

It felt like one day I was a graduate student going to class and studying for exams, and the next I was dropped in the middle of a jungle—where there was a war going on. My job was to provide daily intelligence to higher-ups so informed decisions could be made about creating targets.

I had been recruited in graduate school to be an overseas operations officer. It took over a year and a half of interviews before I officially got hired. I was what is known as a "blue border"—that was the highest level of security classification in the entire U.S. government, established by the director of federal intelligence. That basically boils down to the fact that we were working on the most top-secret stuff. All of our documents had a blue border around the edges, signaling their importance and secrecy.

Every situation guys like us get sent into is different, and I think I survived that war in the jungle because the veterans showed me the ropes. They knew what they were doing and what to watch out for. It was incredibly dangerous, our conditions were crude, and we had to be prepared to defend ourselves at all times. Just being there, you were taking your life in your own hands.

The first thing I was told was that we could be hit by shells any second, so I listened up when the guys who had been there awhile told me what to do. I was told that if there's mortar fire I should always assume there would be more than one. After the first hit, you had to be careful, because it would be easy to run right to the spot where the next one was going to land. Other than that, the advice was simple. If the mortar hits behind you, move forward. If it hits to the left, move to the right.

There were millions of mines out there, and you always had to be careful where you stepped. One of the hardest things I heard was that if you see a bunch of kids playing with an unexploded artillery shell, you have to run. Sadly, there would be no time to warn the

kids—you'd just be blown up with them. If I hadn't listened to the guys who had been out there longer than
I was, I would have been killed. One
day I was walking around when I
nearly stepped on a box and I heard
someone scream, "Don't! Watch
out!" I was about to step on an entire box of unexploded beer can
mines. That would have been it for
me. That experience taught me to always pay attention to people who've been in an area longer than you
have. They know things about the area that can save
your life. Never show up acting like you know everything. Stay alert, listen, and learn.

> **Always pay attention to people who've been in an area longer than you have.**

CHAPTER FIVE

STEALING A TOP-SECRET HOLOGRAM FROM THE RUSSIANS

How to Get Anyone to Do What You Want

THE REQUIREMENT: Determine the nature of materials used in holograms located inside advanced missile guidance systems developed by former Warsaw Pact countries and the Soviet Union. Confirm whether holograms are made with dichromated gelatin or more advanced silver halide.

PARTICIPANTS: C/O Jacob Michaelson, known to subject and hereafter referred to as alias JOHN.

Joon Yang, hereafter referred to as alias/krypto HECTOR.

I looked at the requirement and could barely believe what I was reading. The intelligence suggested that the Soviet Union had developed the most accurate missile guidance system to date. It could predict where a missile was going to land within fifty meters, giving the Soviets a major advantage over the United States. If we wanted to keep America safe, we needed to figure out how they were doing it, and time was of the essence. The United States had only one other bit of intelligence: It was suspected that the accuracy had something to do with the hologram embedded inside. Holograms are made with either silver halide or, if they're very sophisticated, dichromated gelatin. My assignment was to figure out which type of hologram the Soviets were using. If I could get that information it would be an important step in helping the United States figure out how the missile guidance system worked.

I didn't have much information to go on. I started looking at the research being done at engineering labs all over the world to see if I could find anyone who might be connected to the Soviet missile guidance system. I found an engineering lab in Seoul, South Korea, that was working with silver halide *and* dichromated gelatin. I felt that familiar flicker of excitement that told me I was on to something. If this lab was working with both holograms, it was possible that the Soviets were using its research. Now for the hard part. I'd need to build a cover, go to Korea, find someone directly involved in the research, befriend him and gain his trust, and get him to spill his secrets at great risk to his own personal safety. It's a delicate process that can take months or even years—but I didn't have that kind of time. The longer it took to crack how the missile guidance system worked, the longer America was in danger.

A LIFE PARALLEL TO THE TRUTH

I always build my own cover—I never let anyone else do it for me. I'm a spy, but I also have a background in physics. This background helps a lot when I'm trying to recruit a potential target. I can discuss their work intelligently, and ask the right questions. This is why I craft a cover that runs parallel to my own life. It helps me behave in a more natural manner—and that's crucial when you're recruiting someone. Pretending to be something that's totally out of your realm is a recipe for disaster. I'm not going to say I'm a pilot, because if someone asks me the wrong question about how to fly a plane my cover will immediately be blown. I'm going to say I'm a researcher from an engineering firm in the United States—keep it basic. I also like to think about every aspect of my life as this new person, and I always make sure I know how to answer certain questions:

What does he find interesting?

Who will he need to impress?

What topics should he be well versed in?

How does he talk?

What kind of hand gestures does he use?

How does he wear his hair?

What kind of shoes does he wear?

What does he eat?

It might sound dramatic, but for me getting ready to go undercover is kind of like the process of transforming into a mythical vampire. If you're doing it right, you are slowly but surely transforming into another creature. I don't want to go out in the field until I really believe I am that person. If I do this, I know I'll succeed. If I don't, sooner or later I'll make a mistake and get caught. If I can, I'll take a polygraph under my new cover. If I can answer question after question while really being grilled as my new persona, I know I'm ready for anything.

FAVORITE SPY TOOL: A LEGEND THAT CAN BEAT THE POLYGRAPH TEST

Beating a polygraph isn't necessarily easy to do, and I'm not suggesting that a regular person can do it. It's very difficult. However, all seasoned polygraphers will say they can make anyone fail a polygraph. And while that's true, it also means that the person taking the polygraph can manipulate the test on their end too. There are essentially two categories of people who can beat the polygraph:

1. Psychopaths and pathological liars who are also experienced criminals.
2. A trained and experienced case officer who has had at least ten years working a cover legend. This person would be conducting foreign operations for long periods of time—living each day as that cover. I'm not talking for a few days or even weeks. I mean months or years.

I usually worked with six to ten different cover legends, and I designed all of them myself. I succeeded in becoming a different person, however slight, in each case. Now, based on that, assume that one of these legends was one of a pure, kind, innocent individual who never seriously did anything wrong in their entire life. If you are really living this legend, you will beat the polygraph. You will pass every question you are asked. Again, this *is not* easy to do. Most people will not be able to do it, but a spy who's seasoned in cover ops can.

MEETING HECTOR

PERSONALIA:

NAME/KRYPTO: HECTOR

AGE: 44

HT/WT: 5'6", 130 LB

HAIR: Black, short, neat

GLASSES: Yes

PERSONALITY/DEAMEANOR/ATTRIBUTES: Outgoing, energetic, very popular, especially with students, enjoys socializing with students regularly, spends money. Enjoys their attention. Wears well-tailored suits and has an expensive wristwatch.

NATIONALITY/CITIZENSHIP: Korean

KNOWN LANGUAGES: Korean, Japanese, English

PROCLIVITIES: Socializing, drinking, staying out late regularly

FAMILY: Wife XXXXX (35), daughter XXXXXXXX (17), daughter XXXX (14)

ADDRESS: XXX, XXX, XXXX, Seoul, South Korea

TELEPHONE NUMBER: XXX-XXX-XXXX

Leads development work pointed me toward HECTOR. HECTOR was a well-liked professor and researcher at an engineering lab who was working with holograms. Many of his students waited patiently after class for an opportunity to talk with him about their work. It wasn't unusual for these conversations to move to a local café or restaurant. Students were always thrilled to share a meal with the professor, and these dinners often included lots of drinking and went on late into the night. The tradition in the academic community was that the professor always picked up the check. It would be unheard of to let students pay. After hours of drinking and eating, you can imagine that these bills would be fairly big. As a researcher and professor, HECTOR probably made a decent living, but he was far from wealthy. HECTOR was spending lots of time, and possibly a good portion of his paycheck, entertaining his students. I thought maybe HECTOR would enjoy being taken out for once.

THE INTRODUCTION

DATE, TIME, & PLACE OF CONTACT: June, 24, 19XX, 8:00 p.m., XXXXXX Restaurant, Seoul, South Korea.

There was a small window of time after his afternoon lecture when HECTOR was alone in his office. I'd have about ten or twelve minutes before his students came in, so I'd have to make a really good impression quickly. I explained I worked for an engineering firm in America, and we liked to keep updated on research going on around the world. I slipped in a couple of carefully prepared questions about HECTOR's work so that he could see I was knowledgeable on the subject. HECTOR clearly loved talking about his research. As he was telling me about a recent project, I was subtly scanning everything in HECTOR's office, looking for clues about his personality and interests. I saw he had art books mixed in with his academic texts. I made a mental note to look up the artists. When I saw that students were starting to show up outside the office,

I asked him to dinner. "Professor, I'd love to continue this conversation. But I see you have something else to do right now. Could we possibly discuss this further over dinner? It just happens I'm available tonight if you are." I'd found some of the best restaurants in the area while doing my casing, and I suggested an expensive steakhouse and a traditional French restaurant. I was confident in my ability to get that first meeting, so assuming he'd say yes, I made reservations at both. It was a good thing I did, because HECTOR agreed to meet me. My op was off to a good start.

THINK LIKE A SPY: ANTICIPATE

JOHN knew that part of the lure to getting HECTOR to have dinner with him that evening was the suggestion of eating at a well-respected, expensive restaurant. JOHN anticipated that HECTOR would say yes, so he prepared by making reservations at the restaurants in advance. If HECTOR had agreed to have dinner with JOHN and then JOHN discovered it was impossible to get a table, he would have seriously damaged his chances of developing JOHN. Always anticipate potential outcomes and prepare for each one.

THE FIRST MEET, AND IF ALL GOES WELL, A SECOND

DATE, TIME, & PLACE OF CONTACT: June, 24, 19XX, 8:00 p.m., XXXXXX Restaurant, Seoul, South Korea.

The restaurant I chose was extravagant and elegant, and would surely make an impression on HECTOR. I went all-out and ordered an expensive bottle of wine as well as scallops, lobster, duck, desserts, and more wine. A spy has a few objectives with that first meeting. I wanted to develop a good rapport with HECTOR—I wanted him to like me and feel comfortable around me. I wanted to create a sense of obligation, so he'd feel like he had to see me again. And most importantly, I needed to leave with another meeting already set up. I asked lots of questions about his work. It obviously made HECTOR feel important to talk about his research. I also started to piece together some details about the work he was doing. I was very anxious to find out what kind of holograms he worked with, and *who* he worked with. He mentioned a researcher whose name sounded Hungarian—definitely promising. I memorized the name and would pass it along to the analyst working the case to see what else he could find out about this guy.

We talked about interests and art too. (I had researched the art books I'd seen in HECTOR's office.) It seemed like we were two potential business associates getting to know each other, but I was carefully observing the professor. What motivated him? What were his vulnerabilities? What made him tick? I saw that I was right about HECTOR enjoying fine food—especially when someone else was paying. He praised the dinner courses and seemed knowledgeable about wine. I also learned that HECTOR had a daughter who wanted to attend an elite women's college in the United States. HECTOR said it would reflect really well on his family if his daughter could attend such a prestigious school. This was definitely information I could use to my advantage.

At the end of a very long meal—over three hours—I explained that my company in America gave me a substantial allowance to take out "important researchers," emphasizing that I thought HECTOR *was important*. I paid the check and casually mentioned that there was a great steakhouse that I was anxious to try if he'd like to join me. Not about to pass up another terrific free meal, or opportunity to talk about his research, the professor readily agreed. We set up a date for a couple of weeks later. This was a good sign. It's been my experience that if I can get the second meet, I'll eventually get what I need from the target.

RAPPORT/ACCESSIBILITY/SUSCEPTIBILITY

During a prearranged meeting at XXXXXX Restaurant, Seoul, South Korea, case officer told HECTOR that he worked for an American engineering firm looking to swap information, and he had an allowance to buy dinner for people doing interesting research. HECTOR enjoys fine food and wine, though likely can't afford it. Also likes talking about his research at length. He seems to enjoy feeling important and responds well to flattery. He mentioned several trips he has taken to Hungary and the Soviet Union for research purposes. He has a college-age daughter who wants to go to an elite school in America. HECTOR feels it would be a great honor for his family to have a child go to such a prestigious school.

THE RECRUITMENT BEGINS

DATE, TIME, & PLACE OF CONTACT: August 15, 19XX, 8:00 p.m., XXXXXX XXX Restaurant, Seoul, South Korea.

The analyst told me that the intelligence I had given him about the Hungarian researcher was "of value." HECTOR might be the connection we were looking for, and I needed to continue working him. Luckily I had the perfect carrot, and I was planning to dangle it over very expensive steaks at dinner that night.

"Wouldn't you know it? I remembered that I have a friend who is a professor at XXXXX College. Isn't that where your daughter is hoping to go? Perhaps I could make a call on your behalf?"

I got just the reaction I hoped for. The professor's eyes lit right up. The truth was I didn't know anyone at XXXXX College, and the guys back home were figuring out how the heck to pull this off. But that didn't matter right now. I'd offered HECTOR something irresistible, and it was going to keep him coming back. Hopefully, knowing I had a connection to the college his daughter wanted to go to would encourage him to provide me with even more valuable information. The development of HECTOR was now well under way.

Over the next few months we continued to share meals together. Our conversations had deepened, and a real bond started to develop. I don't believe in seduction for seduction's sake. You can't just use people. If you don't actually care about your recruit on some level, you're not going to succeed. You're not going to get the information you need. I'd learned more about HECTOR's research during this time too. As I originally suspected, HECTOR had been doing some work with Hungarian engineers. It also seemed more likely that the Hungarians were sharing this research with the Soviets. All of this information had been ranked as "valuable." Soon the paperwork arrived. This meant I could start paying HECTOR for his information, making him an actual spy for the U.S. government. The next time I saw HECTOR I told him I had some really good news. The information he was sharing was so valuable that I was able to give him a consulting fee. "The work you're doing is *so important*. You really deserve this money." Right now the professor was very happy. In addition to lavish dinners, the professor was thrilled to be receiving extra money. But I knew that very soon I'd need to tell him the truth, and how would he feel then?

HOW INTELLIGENCE IS RANKED

The intelligence gathered by case officers is subject to a very specific ranking system. Note that it's the information, not the source, that's being graded. A case officer's life is based on the value of the information they get. In turn, that value then gives credibility to your source.

- ▶ <u>No value:</u> Nothing can be gained from this information. It's useless.
- ▶ <u>Low value:</u> There is a seed of information, but much more needs to be gathered.
- ▶ <u>Of value:</u> Most of the information case officers gather falls into this category. Of value intelligence is enough to keep your operation going—you'll still get the money for your operation and to pay your source. This is a C+ in the intelligence world, and you always want to go higher than this. It's always a good idea to

know the analyst you're working with, but when you're getting "of value" intelligence it's especially important. An analyst might deem your information "of value"—but then tell you through back channels that it's actually "low value" and he'll tell you what you need to get in order to kick things up a notch. Your analyst would do this just so you can keep going and do better. The analyst may ask you to come see him, so that he can explain to you what's going on . . . or he may have ideas about who you should contact. Sometimes you'll end up with a "quarterback operation." That's when you take the analyst with you, and he can meet the source you're working with.

- ▶ <u>High value:</u> This is information that's good, and actually causes decision makers to consider changing policy—but not enough to actually change the policy.
- ▶ <u>Of major significance:</u> This is what every case officer wants to get. This kind of intelligence is incredibly important, and as a result changes the policy of the United States toward another country. Getting "of major sig" makes you well known throughout the world of ops, and you get a handsome bonus for each major significance you obtain.

DROPPING THE FIG LEAF

DATE, TIME, & PLACE OF CONTACT: October, 12, 19XX, 8:00 p.m., XXX XXXX Restaurant, Seoul, South Korea.

Things just kept getting better for HECTOR. He was very excited when he showed up at our next meeting with some big news. His daughter just got accepted to XXXXX College. HECTOR was very grateful that I'd used my influence to help—but I was just relieved the people back home were able to pull the right strings. I'd been consistently getting good intelligence from HECTOR, and I wanted to keep it coming. Helping his daughter get into college was definitely going to help. I started to sense that our relationship was reaching a critical point. In almost every op there's a moment when you can tell the recruit has a pretty clear idea about why he's really getting paid for his information, and that the mysterious American company is actually the U.S. government. He just needs to hear the truth, and you've got to give it to him. I call it the "dropping-the-fig-leaf moment." My intuition tends to lead me to the right moment for the big reveal. I try not to make a big deal out of it. I'll usually just hand over the "consulting fee" and say something like, "It feels really good to be a spy, doesn't it?" I get the same response nearly every time . . . "I like it, it is very, very exciting." It's amazing how many regular people love being a spy. Now that everything was out in the open and HECTOR was "witting," I could give him direct requests for information, or "tasking." I could also brief HECTOR before his trips to Hungary, and debrief him when he got back.

BIG NEWS, A NEAR MISS, AND A RUINED SUIT

DATE, TIME, & PLACE OF CONTACT: December 3, 19XX, 7:00 p.m., XXXX XX Restaurant, Seoul, South Korea.

I was debriefing HECTOR about his latest trip to Hungary one night when I learned something very interesting. HECTOR said a Hungarian researcher wanted to show him something. HECTOR was stunned when the researcher led him to a glass display case holding a hologram. *The* hologram—the very one the American government desperately wanted information about. It was sitting right there in a lab in Hungary. This was big news, and I was very anxious to get in touch with the analyst back home.

I always run an SDR while I head back from a meeting. I was a few blocks in when I noticed the sound of footsteps behind me. It was late at night, and the usually packed streets of Seoul were less crowded, for once. The sound grew closer, so I made a turn that enabled me to look back. There were three guys walking behind me. I crossed the street, and the three men stayed on their side. Because I was always casing, I knew an alternate route and I decided to turn on the next street. About a block later, the guys were back and they were right behind me. Now I knew I was about to be mugged— or worse, busted for being a spy. I had to escape. You never want to fight three guys at once if you don't have to. I started walking quickly in the other direction, but one of the men started running after me. I started running in the direction of the Han River, and he was still coming after me. But he didn't expect what I did next. I jumped right into the river. It was really dark, and I was treading water as quietly as I could, and this guy couldn't see me at all. I was hoping he'd just give up.

Eventually I heard the sound of footsteps walking away. He was gone. I patiently treaded water a bit longer, and when I thought it was safe I found a place to climb out. I was wet, cold, and I'd ruined my best suit. But I knew that didn't matter. I was still alive and I hadn't compromised my op.

BONUS TIP

You want to avoid a fight if you can, but sometimes it's not an option. This is why you have to know critical self-defense tactics. Remember, to see what spies use, visit www.SpyCombatives.com.

THE BIG COUP

The analyst was just as excited as I was about the new intelligence HECTOR gave me about the hologram. This might be the big break we were looking for. But the analyst wanted something else, and it was going to be difficult and dangerous to pull off. The analyst wanted HECTOR and me to figure out how to get our hands on the actual hologram so the United States could analyze it. If we did this, the intelligence would be considered "of major significance"—the highest rating an intelligence officer can get. The idea was to somehow ship the hologram to the United States, where scientists would remove a scraping for analysis. I wanted to get the hologram, but I also knew I'd be putting HECTOR in a very dangerous position. What if the Hungarians saw the scraping? What if it got lost or damaged? Or they figured out it was missing? If anything happened to the hologram, HECTOR would most likely be killed. The analyst assured me the scraping would be so minute, only the world's most powerful microscopes would be able to notice. When I told HECTOR about what the United States wanted us to do, he was game. He felt the world would be safer if the United States could figure out how the Soviet missile detection system worked.

Our next step was to convince the Hungarians that HEC-TOR should have the hologram temporarily. HECTOR simply told his Hungarian colleagues that he'd like to borrow it for research purposes, and that having the hologram would be a very useful learning experience for his students. We were relieved when the Hungarians agreed. But we were nervous too. Getting the scraping from the hologram was a major operation that involved nearly a hundred people from the U.S. intelligence world. U.S. intelligence officers dressed like visiting professors had a "meeting" with HECTOR at his lab. Inside their briefcases were special materials to safely pack up the hologram for transport to the United States. Meanwhile, a Concorde was fueling up, preparing to fly the hologram to a secret Air Force base in the United States. There was so much that could go wrong. The Hungarians or KGB could get wind of what we were doing. The hologram could get damaged, something could happen to the plane. The list went on and on, and we prepared the best we could for every possibility. We had to keep in mind that if anything went wrong, HECTOR's life would be in serious danger. I knew I wouldn't breathe a sigh of relief until that hologram was back in HECTOR's office—in one piece.

Somehow, miraculously, everything went exactly as planned. The hologram made it to the United States, where scientists were able to take a microscopic scraping for analysis. The hologram was packed up, put back on the Concorde, and was on display in HECTOR's lab just twenty-four hours later. No one had any idea the hologram had taken a journey to the United States, and no one ever knew that this mild-mannered Korean researcher had actually been collecting big secrets for the American government.

YOUR INNER SPY

The Art of Elicitation: Who Do You Want to Recruit?

Most foreign spies are recruited because they have access or knowledge that the government finds desirable, or they are able to travel in and out of certain areas without raising suspicion. For example, the jazz singer Josephine Baker was very popular in Europe when World War II started, and she was able to smuggle messages written in invisible ink to Axis sympathizers on her sheet music. Famous playwright Noël Coward used his access to rich and powerful Americans to pass along top-secret information to President Roosevelt. You don't have to be a celebrity to be a spy either—in the 1980s, a secretary working for the West German President was arrested when she was discovered spying for East Germany. College professors, engineers, and even secretaries potentially have access to valuable information that might appeal to a foreign government.

Your average American isn't likely to be recruited as a spy. However, there are often times when we need to ally with someone in the real world—whether it's in business, or with a neighbor, or with someone at your child's school—and understanding the process can make your efforts much more successful.

TACTIC #1: FIRST IMPRESSIONS ARE EVERYTHING—DEVELOP A GOOD RAPPORT

JOHN didn't just barge into HECTOR's office and introduce himself the day he arrived. Observation is important, and he would have noted as much as he could about HECTOR's general habits and behavior before making an introduction. What makes this guy tick? What are his vulnerabilities? Any intelligence officer knows that the introduction is a big moment, and you can't mess it up. The goal of that introduction is to present yourself as an interesting enough person that you'll leave having the "first meet" already set up. JOHN would have known that he would have just a few minutes to impress HECTOR enough that he'd want to have dinner with him. JOHN went in knowing exactly what to ask about HECTOR's research, chatted a bit about good restaurants, and maybe even mentioned what it's like to have kids old enough to apply to college. Everything JOHN did in that introductory meeting was done with the mind-set of setting up another meet.

In the intelligence world, a good rapport goes a long way. If you don't have a good rapport with someone right off the bat, you will not be able to recruit this person or elicit information from him. It is crucial to come off as likable—*immediately*. The subject has to connect with you and feel interested in spending time with you. This is another thing Hollywood gets wrong. If you want to get someone on your side, you don't sit across a table from them yelling, cursing, and pounding your fist. That's interrogation, and it's not going to work when you're hoping to

recruit someone. When building a rapport with a potential recruit, it's important to avoid the following behaviors.

Behaviors That Damage Rapport

- Don't come across as judgy. Avoid statements like, "I
  don't get why you would do or think that."
- Avoid giving advice. What people want is approval. You
  want to say something along the lines of, "That was a
  smart move," rather than, "You should do it this way."
- Don't be the person who has to win the argument—let
  the target win.
- Don't be a one-upper. If the target tells you about his
  biggest sales coup, don't top it with a story about how
  you actually sold more.
- Avoid interrupting the target when they're speaking.
- Never downgrade their status or profession.
- Never finish their sentences for them.

TACTIC #2: USE THE "WEAPONS OF MASS INFLUENCE," OR RASCLS—RECIPROCATION, AUTHORITY, SCARCITY, CONSISTENCY (ALSO COMMITMENT), LIKING, AND SOCIAL PROOF

Human beings are complicated. Since there is no one foolproof
method for recruiting and eliciting information, intelligence officers use RASCLS, the six "weapons of mass influence" designed
by psychologist Robert Cialdini. The idea here is that because we
are constantly bombarded by different sights, sounds, and smells,
our brains developed some "fixed action patterns of behavior."
This means that when we encounter a specific situation we tend

to react in a certain way. If we were constantly analyzing stimuli, our brains would just freeze up and we wouldn't be able to function. These patterns help us respond to what's going on around us. However, intelligence officers (as well as many criminals, unfortunately) understand how these patterns work, and can manipulate the following behaviors to their advantage.

Reciprocation

Intelligence officers are taught to "give something to get something," and that's what we mean when we talk about reciprocation. When you give a person something early on in a relationship, it usually creates a sense of obligation. This could be something minor—like buying someone a cup of coffee, or maybe sharing an important business contact. Or it could be something much bigger, like how JOHN helped get HECTOR's daughter into college. Either way, a sense of obligation is established and you're setting up a scenario where the other person is likely to want to return the favor.

Authority

When JOHN was building his cover, he purposefully created a role that put him in a position of authority. He was a "physicist from an engineering firm in America with a big expense account." This would suggest that JOHN was an important person, that he had influence, and that his power might extend to HECTOR in some way. JOHN was also sure to dress the part as well. His designer suits and penchant for expensive restaurants all supported the idea that he was a person of authority. In the intelligence world, that air of authority also plays a big role in the recruitment cycle. Once JOHN recruited HECTOR and had him on the payroll, JOHN's authority would help create a feeling of obligation. HECTOR would feel obligated to get intelligence for JOHN. Spying is dangerous, and HECTOR would also need to feel confident in JOHN's knowledge of tradecraft—since HECTOR would essentially be putting himself in JOHN's hands. JOHN's coming off as authoritative helps assuage any fear HECTOR may have about his own safety.

Scarcity

People are drawn to things that are rare or scarce. That restaurant in town where it's nearly impossible to get a reservation? That's usually the place where people want to eat. And if you've ever passed on an item in a store, only to feel regretful about it when you find out it's no longer available—that's scarcity. When recruiting a target, an intelligence officer will dangle a carrot—perhaps doing a favor such as helping a family member—but then make it clear the offer will quickly go away. A recruit has to act quickly if they want to reap the benefit.

Consistency and Commitment

We don't trust people who aren't consistent, that's just common sense. If an intelligence officer doesn't exhibit consistent behavior with a potential recruit, he won't get anywhere. Commitment during the development phase can actually mean making small connections. It might mean agreeing on a particular subject. For instance, HECTOR may have agreed with JOHN that both of their countries would be safer thanks to the information HECTOR was providing. They are both committing to the *same idea*. This also creates an environment that makes the recruit more comfortable. If HECTOR sees that he and JOHN share the same ideas about national security, he may feel compelled to open up and share more secrets about other things.

Liking

"Liking" obviously goes back to rapport—and an intelligence officer needs to start working on rapport during that first introduction. But it doesn't stop there. An intelligence officer must continue to look for additional ways to develop a bond with a recruit. What traits do they have in common? What interests do they share? Can they swap notes about raising children, hobbies, or other personal interests? For this process to be the most successful, the relationship needs to move from "liking" to "friend" to feeling like "this is the only person in the world who really understands me."

Social Proof

Whether we like it or not, there are certain things that signal a person's place in society. Pulling up in a limo suggests wealth and importance. If loads of people are lining up to get coffee from a particular coffee shop, you assume the coffee is really good. In the espionage world, an intelligence officer can use social proof to make a recruit feel more comfortable about what he's doing. An intelligence officer might show his importance by getting impossible-to-get tickets to a hit show, or the best table at an exclusive restaurant. Another way social proof is used is to make the recruit feel comfortable by letting him know he's not the only person who has done what he's doing. A case officer might say, "Oh, when I was working with X, he used to bring me reports about x, y and z." This shows a recruit that others have successfully managed to pull off what he is about to do.

TACTIC #3: ELICITATION 101

The Art of Elicitation

The art of elicitation involves manipulating a conversation so that the target starts to give away information that's of great interest, without necessarily realizing he's done so. JOHN brilliantly used elicitation to develop a relationship with HECTOR. JOHN used HECTOR's love of expensive meals and his desire to get his daughter into an elite school to curry favor with him. When done well, elicitation is so subtle that the target will likely have no idea what's happening.

Obviously, intelligence officers are highly trained in elicitation techniques, but often savvy businesspeople and even criminals use elicitation to their advantage. Chances are, you've probably used elicitation without even knowing it. If you asked your wife some subtle questions to figure out what she wants for her birthday, that's a very simple example of elicitation. (To watch a video case study of elicitation and how you can use this skill to get almost anything you want, visit www.SurviveLike aSpy.com.)

Unfortunately, not everyone who uses elicitation is doing so for such innocent purposes. A shady business associate may use elicitation to extract information about your business to get an advantage over you. Or even worse, criminals use elicitation to trick you into divulging important personal information like your PIN or Social Security number. Being aware of some of the main elicitation techniques can prevent you from being scammed or spilling secrets to your business's competition. With patience and practice, you can also use these techniques to pull information you want from someone else.

Playing Dumb

"I'm new to this. I have no idea how this works!"

A person trying to elicit information might just play dumb. They may act like they have no idea what they're doing. Knowing that human beings are helpful by nature, they know someone is likely to jump in and help, ultimately giving them the exact information they need. A person might say something like, "I didn't know this place designs software for the U.S. government," to which someone may very well respond, "Yes, we've been making x, y, and z for years"—divulging the information that person wants to know.

Flattery

"Wow! I bet you played a key role in this project!"

The old adage "flattery will get you nowhere" is definitely not true in the intelligence world. It can actually get you quite far. A person trying to elicit information might make a flattering statement, and then sit back and wait for you to fill in the blanks about what you really did. A slightly less direct route might be saying something like, "I bet only a handful of people really know how this actually works," to which an average person will most likely volunteer that they, indeed, are one of the few who *do* know.

Common Interests

"That's a nice car you drive. You like cars? You've got to see the vintage Mustang I'm restoring. You should come by and check it out."

Someone trying to elicit information from you may attempt to connect with you over a common interest. They may cite that common interest as a way to convince you there's something you need to see—or there's somewhere you'd love to go. If you agree to this, you've just assented to continuing the relationship outside of the initial meeting place, putting the person in a good position to develop a relationship with you further.

The False Statement

"Everyone knows that Iran doesn't have the technology to build a weapon of mass destruction."

A person trying to elicit information may hope that you'll respond to a false statement they make. Humans are wired to want to appear knowledgeable and have a tendency to want to correct inaccurate information. Delivering false statements tends to prompt people to answer with correct information. If you're on the receiving end of a false proclamation, simply listen and don't respond. Resist the temptation to set the speaker straight.

The Good Listener

"Are you okay? You don't seem yourself right now."

Elicitation requires patience. If a person presents himself as a good listener, eventually you may open up about a topic that's appealing to him. He may also validate your feeling to encourage you to do this—hoping you'll open up about a problem at work.

Word Repetition

"My team is just under so much pressure to meet this big deadline."

This involves encouraging a person to expand on something he just said by repeating a portion of that person's statement. If you're complaining about work being extra-tough, you might be asked, "Oh, what's going on at work?" When you respond, "It's tough because my boss is being a jerk lately," the questioner may follow up with, "What's going on, that he's being a jerk?" To which you respond that he's being a jerk because you're under deadline to deliver a big project . . . giving your questioner all the specifics. Watch out for parroted words and phrases. They could signal that the person you're speaking with is playing you. Don't fall for it.

Be Aware of Sharing Knowledge When You Shouldn't

If you're talking to someone at a business function, and he's showing off his knowledge about a topic that you know a lot about—maybe software development or security systems—it's easy to feel that if this guy already knows about this stuff, you can talk about what you know. You might think, "What harm can it do? He already knows about it." You find yourself saying something like this:

"I can see you know a lot about security systems, so I might as well tell you."

The truth might be that he doesn't actually know anything—until now, because you just filled him in, and that's exactly what he was hoping you would do.

SOMEONE IS TRYING TO ELICIT INFORMATION FROM ME. NOW WHAT?

Imagine you're traveling for work. You've had a long day of meetings and you decide to treat yourself to a drink at the bar and catch some of the game. There's another businessman sitting next to you. You're cheering for the same team and you end up chatting. It turns out he's in a similar business, and you start to swap stories. Before you even realize it, you've told him more than you should have about an upcoming product your company is working on. It might be innocent. Or, one of your competitors has just elicited very useful information from you. It's never easy to tell the difference between a casual conversation and elicitation, and to complicate things people generally want to be polite. If you ever think someone is trying to trick you into revealing information that should remain private, try the following:

- ▶ Make it clear you don't have the information. Just tell them, "I don't know."
- ▶ Deflect the question by asking one yourself: "I don't know, why do you ask?"
- ▶ Give a vague, generic answer that doesn't actually reveal any information.
- ▶ Refer them to a public source: "I think that's on our website."
- ▶ Change the topic immediately.

SPY ENCOUNTERS: ALEX
GETTING JACKED UP BY FOREIGN POLICE

Getting stopped by foreign police can really mess up an operation, so I always had to be very careful about how I behaved whenever that happened. I spent many years working in Asia—and I have gotten stopped by the police in Seoul and Tokyo. I always knew that the number one way to mess up would be to carry a gun. You just can't do that, especially in Japan. It completely goes against their culture, and if caught you could land in jail for a very long time. I learned that the best way to deal with the foreign police was to act polite, answer their questions quickly—but not to act like I was in a big hurry; that made them suspicious of my motives. I was always sure to speak English, even though my Japanese is very good. I wanted it to be clear that I was from a foreign country, and it's less likely that they would mess with an American. Usually they'd be satisfied with my answers and they'd let me go on my way.

One time, I was casing out a quiet residential neighborhood in Japan, when the police stopped me. They started questioning me very heavily, and I got the feeling they were not going to let me go so easily. I was starting to get nervous, because it would really mess things up for me if they decided to take me in. I'm not proud of it, but I started answering their questions in a manner that may have suggested I was an afflicted person. I just acted confused, and smiled a lot, and nodded my head. I honestly wanted them to think I was not very bright, or "not all there." It worked. The police came to the conclusion that I was harmless and they left me alone.

CHAPTER SIX

SNATCHING AND GRABBING A NARCO-TERRORIST

How to Survive a Kidnapping

THE REQUIREMENT: Confirm the true identity of X, an individual believed to be a lead figure in a drug ring. X is traveling into the United States using the identity of XXXX XXXXX of New York, NY, a U.S. citizen. Once identity is confirmed, X will be subject to extraordinary rendition, removed from his native country, and brought to undisclosed location.

PARTICIPANTS: C/O Trevor McDonnell, hereafter referred to as alias CHAD.

C/O Robert Darby, hereafter referred to as alias ETHAN.

C/O Linda Patterson, hereafter referred to as alias ANNA.

TARGET: Mateo Sanchez, hereafter referred to as alias/krypto WINDSOR.

TRADING YOUR LIFE FOR "PARADISE"

Imagine the following scenario: Someone approaches you and asks if you'd like to live in the Bahamas. That sounds pretty good to you, but then the offer gets better. The house is paid for—it won't cost you anything—and they'll give you a couple of million dollars too. Sounds great, right? But there's more. In exchange for a house in paradise and a large sum of cash, you'll have to give something in return: *your identity*. They'll want your birth certificate, driver's license, passport, Social Security number, and bank information. Actually, they want to get down to the essence of who you really are, so they'll take your computer too. You just need to stop being you and say goodbye to your friends and community.

Now that you know the real story, you don't want to do it. That's when they say, "Oh, well. I hope your kids will be okay walking home from school every day." Terrified for their lives, you realize you don't have much choice. The person you hand everything over to is likely associated with a serious criminal. You hope your kids will be safe in your new life. And your old life? Your identity is now being assumed by a major narcotics dealer. He's become you. He'll use your Social Security number and bank account, and having your passport means he can travel freely between his native country and the United States whenever he wants.

COLLAPSING THE CHAIN

DATE, TIME, & PLACE OF CONTACT: January 21, 19XX, XXX XXXXX Street, Bogotá, Colombia.

<u>PERSONALIA:</u>

NAME/KRYPTO: WINDSOR

AGE: 39

HT/WT: 5'8", 175 LB

HAIR: Black with streaks of gray, long in back, thinning

GLASSES: No

PERSONALITY/DEMEANOR/ATTRIBUTES: Highly intelligent, cunning, can win over people when necessary. Known to be brutal.

NATIONALITY/CITIZENSHIP: Colombian, Colombia

KNOWN LANGUAGES: Spanish, English

FAMILY: Parents deceased, brother XXXXXX (38), brother XXXXXX (35)

GIRLFRIEND: XXXX XXXXXX (26), XXXX XXXXXX (32)

ADDRESS: XXXX XXXXX, Bogotá, Columbia; XXXX XXXXX, New York, New York

It might sound hard to believe, but it's true that criminals from other nations are willing to pay large sums of money for an American identity to continue their work as the most brutal and violent drug dealers in the world. We call them narco-terrorists. These guys are the worst of the worst. Some narco-terrorists are so sadistic, they treat the people working for them like animals—these people will be working in the crops or factories completely naked, so there's no chance they can escape or steal. The ability to travel freely between America and the native country where the rest of the drug ring is located means this narco-terrorist is transporting drugs and money into the United States, and killing lots of people in the process.

It was my job to lead a team that stops this from happening, and we were after WINDSOR, who we believed to be the top "narco-terrorist" in the drug chain. Our ultimate goal was to "break the chain." That means we're clamping down on the entire operation from end to end to stop it for once and for all. We'd need to know where the drugs were being grown, and all the players involved. Part of the team would map out where the drugs were going. Other parts would figure who was driving the trucks, and who the lowlifes were who sold the drugs outside of schools. If we didn't collapse the entire chain from end to end, and just went after a few key individuals, a new person would just pop up to replace the guy we took out. That doesn't solve the problem, because in the world of drug dealing there's always another WINDSOR.

THINK LIKE A SPY: ALWAYS EXAMINE THE BIGGER PICTURE

While it seems that taking out a major drug dealer like WINDSOR will solve a big problem—like illegal drugs being brought over our borders into America—it's only one part of the story. Because these guys have worked hard to figure out the big picture, they know the problem won't be solved for good until other elements of the situation are also dealt with. While it's often tempting to focus on one problem, make sure you are looking closely at the entire situation to determine if there are larger issues that also need to be conquered. What other challenges might arise? Who else is involved? What actions need to be taken to solve the problem for once and for all?

So, while the big goal was to break down the entire chain, my specific job was to work with others to take out the bad guy. In this case that was WINDSOR, who was easily flying in and out of the United States on an illegally purchased passport. This part of the process is called "extraordinary rendition," and it's dangerous and difficult. This is because the end result is kidnapping our target, and getting him out of the United States for good. It's also politically challenging. No foreign country likes their citizens being snatched up by the United States, especially when it happens on their turf. That's why we spend months, if not years, being incredibly careful and collecting lots of information. We have to be sure we're focused on the right person, and there is no room for mistakes.

MAKING SURE, AND MAKING SURE AGAIN, BEFORE WE GO IN

DATE, TIME, & PLACE OF CONTACT: March 17, 19XX, 8:04 p.m., XXXXXXX Restaurant, Bogotá, Colombia.

A drug bust is something TV and movies get completely wrong. In the movies, the good guys swoop in and grab the bad guy. It all happens in a few minutes, and you get little or none of the backstory. The truth is, to pull off something this complicated and delicate, it takes years of training and the expertise of many different people. We just can't risk grabbing the wrong guy—or worse, a completely innocent person. These operations require the expertise of several different entities. It could be the Border Patrol, the CIA, and the NSA all exchanging information, putting together our different pieces like a big puzzle. We'll have drones collecting data, we'll be eavesdropping, checking his phone, and we'll be taking pictures.

After we've gathered all the biographical data, we have to actually collect fingerprints and sometimes DNA. Just getting a simple set of fingerprints takes more planning and work than you might imagine. Because we had been following WINDSOR and watching him for a long time, we knew that he occasionally went to a restaurant in one of the rougher neighborhoods in Bogotá. WINDSOR was no dummy, and remember, he had his own team of people whose job it was to protect him. This meant he had enough sense not to have any regular patterns of behavior. He wasn't going to just show up at the same restaurant at the same time every Tuesday night. He was careful, and that made our job harder. ETHAN, one of my teammates, had been making the rounds, getting to know people in the area—and hanging out at local establishments. That's how we knew there was a chance that eventually WINDSOR could turn up at a few different places, including XXXXXXX Restaurant. We had people watching the different places where WINDSOR might show up, and waited patiently for an opportunity to jump into action. One Friday night I was at home eating dinner when the phone rang. It was ETHAN calling to say that WINDSOR's car had pulled up at XXXXXXX Restaurant. This might be the chance we'd been waiting for. I was out the door in seconds, and picked up our teammate ANNA along the way.

When I got to ANNA's place, she took over the driving, because I couldn't be seen. I'm a big guy, but I stayed low, so it wouldn't look like I was even in the car. The plan was for ANNA to enter the restaurant and order a drink, watching WINDSOR the entire time. If she saw that WINDSOR was busy and engaged and unlikely to walk out to his car any minute, then ANNA would step outside and light up a cigarette. That was my signal to move in and get the prints. ANNA parked in a dark part of the parking lot and went inside the restaurant. I hid behind the car, scanning the area to see if anyone was watching me. About ten minutes later ANNA came out and lit up. We were good to go. Moving as quietly and quickly as possible, I snuck up to WINDSOR's car and affixed some clear, nearly invisible tape, right about where WINDSOR's hand would touch it to open the door. This would give us a set of his fingerprints so we could get a positive ID before we took the big step of snatching him. I had one more thing to do. I affixed a small piece of electrical tape to the left taillight, to help our people keep track of WINDSOR's car. Then I quickly and carefully made my way back to our car, and prepared to wait for ANNA. ANNA came out after finishing her drink and we left. We were glad it went well—*so far*. We wouldn't know if we got a good print until ETHAN retrieved the tape—and that would be an entirely different challenge.

THINK LIKE A SPY: COLLECT ALL THE INFORMATION YOU CAN

It would be a complete disaster to grab the wrong guy. There's just no room for error when pulling off an extraordinary rendition. It's not enough to spy on someone's phone calls or even get their fingerprints. All the data must be examined and collected before a positive identification is made. It's tempting to look to one source of information when trying to make a big decision, but you always want to collect as much information as you can from multiple sources to make the most informed decision possible.

DATE, TIME, & PLACE OF CONTACT: March 17, 19XX, 11:20 p.m., Intersection of XX Street and XX Street, El Bronx, Bogotá, Colombia.

ETHAN needed to retrieve the tape, but he needed to do it without anyone noticing.

That meant ETHAN was in position, watching every move WINDSOR made. It was easier now to follow his car, since ETHAN could identify it by the marking on the taillight. As soon as his car stopped and WINDSOR got out, ETHAN would have to be ready to grab the tape (and hopefully fingerprints) without being seen. If he got caught, things were going to get very messy. ETHAN had his fingers crossed that WINDSOR wasn't headed home for the night (security at his home was tight), but instead that he planned to make another stop, providing an opportunity to retrieve the tape. After driving a few more blocks, WINDSOR parked his car. Luck was on ETHAN's side: WINDSOR was headed into a nightclub. Once ETHAN saw WINDSOR go inside, and could ascertain that he wasn't being watched, he approached WINDSOR's car and took the tape. So far, the operation was a big success.

HEATING UP THE AREA

DATE, TIME, & PLACE OF CONTACT: March 24, 19XX, 9:30 p.m., XXXXXXX Restaurant, Bogotá, Colombia.

ANNA, ETHAN, and I were thrilled when the news came back that the fingerprints ETHAN retrieved matched what our people had on file. But the bottom line was that fingerprints weren't enough. We needed DNA to positively confirm WINDSOR's identity. ETHAN had been making relationships around town, and was doing a great job connecting with different people. It was time for ETHAN to use one of the relationships he built to help get the DNA. This was something we'd only want to do if we knew we were getting really close.

You've got to be careful not to "heat up the area" too much when working an op. While we need to spend lots of time watching people and collecting information, things "heat up" when our people start asking questions. ETHAN had been cultivating a relationship with one of the waitresses. He chatted with her, and knew she was struggling to care for a young child by herself—and that told him money was an issue. As far as he knew, she did not have a relationship with WINDSOR or any of his associates. But if he started asking too many questions or making weird requests, she might get spooked or suspicious. That's why we were extra-careful about getting this last but crucial bit of evidence.

The next time ETHAN saw WINDSOR at XXXXXXX Restaurant, he knew it was time to ask the waitress for help. WINDSOR has been eating and drinking with his associates for a few hours when they all got up to leave. As the waitress was about to clear the table, ETHAN called her over. ETHAN simply told the waitress that he had an easy way for her to earn some money. All she had to do was give him a plate—the one WINDSOR had eaten off of. If she found the request strange, she didn't care once ETHAN offered her $100. Once he had the plate, ETHAN got it to our guys ASAP. They were going to try to get DNA off of any saliva left behind. Once we had that, we'd know for sure if we had a match.

THE SNATCH-AND-GRAB

DATE, TIME, & PLACE OF CONTACT: April 4, 19XX, 9:00 a.m., XX Street, Bogotá, Colombia.

The snatching-and-grabbing of our target was an intense experience, and my heart was always pounding hard in my chest as we were working up to it. We just wanted to get out of the operation in one piece, but we knew WINDSOR's people wanted to hurt us too. And they were all around us. We had been working hard for a long time, we had a plan ready, and everyone on the team understood what his role was. ETHAN had information that WINDSOR was going to be headed to a meeting at approximately nine a.m. Early that morning, our people were monitoring every move he made. Once he headed out, our people started following him. Even though he took back roads, obviously making sure he wasn't being followed, we were able to keep tabs on him without him knowing he was being watched. Our intelligence indicated that the meeting would take place at XX Street, and ETHAN, ANNA, and I would be there waiting with the rest of the team.

THE DISTRACTION THAT GOT US WINDSOR

We knew that a guy like WINDSOR wasn't going to head out to a "business meeting" without his security people. They were going to be armed, and they'd have no problem killing anyone who posed a threat. Obviously this made it difficult for us to get close enough to WINDSOR to actually grab him. This is why we sometimes have to create a big distraction. We had to engineer a situation that would cause enough of a commotion that WINDSOR's people would put their guard down long enough for us to get him.

Our plan was to use a staged car crash. They are so loud—it sounds like a gun being shot—and it works great. It would be environmentally appropriate too, since we wanted to get WINDSOR while he was on the street. If WINDSOR was in a meeting on the eighth floor of a hotel, then obviously that wouldn't work. A car crash was also an event that would reasonably occur in the area; that's important too.

As our guys on the ground confirmed that WINDSOR was getting closer to the location, we got ready to create "the distraction." Car A was parked near the building we expected WINDSOR to enter. Car B was held farther up the street, ready to head directly into the action when signaled. There were so many things going on—communications flying between officers, drones flying above, a van full of CIA officers ready to jump out and grab WINDSOR, and all of us hoping that Cars A and B would be able to connect at just the right time. As WINDSOR's car slowed, Car B was cued to start speeding up toward Car A. Because of some other cars on the street, he had to wait a bit before he headed toward Car A. The path opened up, Car B picked up speed, and Car A was instructed to pull out just as Car B was flying down the road. It couldn't have gone any better. The crash sound was spectacular. Very loud, and sounded much worse than it actually was. And it did just what we needed it to do. As WINDSOR's security people braced themselves for an attack from the left (the crash sounded like possible gunfire), our people immediately moved in from the right. It was crazy, and chaotic, but everyone knew what to do. One of our men grabbed WINDSOR, bagged him, shoved him into a van, and drove him off to an airfield where a private plane was waiting.

It was a successful operation, and it felt great knowing that our hard work as a team was going to keep drugs off of America's streets.

SURPRISE, SPEED, AND VIOLENCE OF ACTION

None of our homework would matter in the end if we didn't react appropriately when the time came to nab WINDSOR. The standard operating procedure is "surprise, speed, and violence of action." Following this procedure is crucial to completing our job.

Surprise

This isn't as simple as it sounds. It's not just about running in on our target when they least expect it (although that's part of it). The main idea here is to finish all of our actions before WINDSOR's people are able to react. This means we're using stealth movements to get as close to our target as possible. This is also important because it means my team is being put in a good position to defend itself once the other guys realize what's happening.

Speed

Obviously we're going to move swiftly—but speed in this case also refers to moving in before the other guys know what's really happening and can attack us back. They might have a plan up their sleeves that they could execute to our detriment. For instance, maybe they have a grenade or a bomb. We have to launch our attack before they can react by launching a counterattack.

Violence of Action

"Violence of action" means to use all strength, speed, surprise, and aggression to fight your enemy. When we're going in to get someone, we are putting our lives on the line. We have to go in full force to increase our chances of getting WINDSOR. This means really going at it with everything we've got. Our survival depends on it. Grabbing someone like WINDSOR is an incredibly intense experience, and anything can happen. When it's gone right, it ends with our getting a bag over his head and loading him onto a plane. This plane isn't your typical plane either. There's no flight plan, and we're purposely flying below the radar and taking off from a private airfield. We're going to take him somewhere—either Guantánamo Bay, or one of the safe facilities the United States has in host countries all around the world. And once we've got him there, we know the world is just a little bit safer for Americans and their families.

YOUR INNER SPY

Extraordinary rendition is about our government snatching some of the worst criminals out there to keep America safe. While extraordinary rendition might be unusual, I'm sad to say that kidnapping is a real concern even for regular people. Many executives and high-net-worth individuals take my training classes because they know there's a chance they could be kidnapped—and if it ever happens they want to survive. Unfortunately, in certain parts of the world, kidnapping is a real danger—regardless of who you are. Americans especially run the risk of being kidnapped in Mexico (where the kidnapping rate is very high), Haiti, Brazil, the Philippines, India, Colombia, and Venezuela. But kidnapping can hit close to home too. Americans watched the news in horror as the story broke about the abduction of thirty-four-year-old mother of two Sherri Papini. Details are still emerging, but Papini was abducted by two women while jogging and suffered horrific beatings and abuse for nearly three weeks. Her abductors threw her eighty-seven-pound body on the side of a California highway, and she was eventually able to flag down a motorcyclist. She had a chain around her waist, she was badly beaten, bruised, branded, and covered in scabs. Her kidnappers had also chopped off her long blond hair.

So what do you do if the unthinkable happens? Maybe you're on vacation when you get pulled over by what you thought were the police, but now there's a gun in your face and you're being screamed at in another language and forced into a van. Or maybe you are using the ATM late at night when you're grabbed from behind. The guy who grabbed you has a weapon out and he's trying to get you into a van or truck. You realize you are about to be kidnapped and you're terrified. While I hope this is something that never happens to you, know that if you are ever the victim of a kidnapping there are some things you can do to increase your chances of being found alive.

TACTIC #1: WEIGH YOUR OPTIONS IN MERE SECONDS

The actual abduction is one of the two most dangerous phases in the kidnapping process. (If you survive the abduction, the rescue will be the other part of the process where you are also at high risk of being killed.) This is because the situation is chaotic—your kidnappers are prepared to use their weapons, and if things don't go their way, there's a chance they will simply kill you. After all, a dead body doesn't fight back.

I've said this before. If someone gets you into a vehicle against your will, there's a good chance that you'll be killed. There will only be seconds to assess the situation. How many people are there? Do they have guns? Is anyone else around who can help? Can you run to safety? If you really believe you can fight off your kidnappers and escape, you should. However, if you don't believe the opportunity to run exists, and fighting them off isn't an option, your best chance for survival is to pay very close attention to what I'm going to teach you in this chapter. Whatever choice you make, you should make as big a commotion as possible before you're put in the transport vehicle. Yell, scream for help, fight, kick—anything that will draw attention to what's happening and make it as obvious as possible that you're being taken.

WHY STAYING CALM MATTERS

Obviously, if you are being kidnapped you're going to be out of your mind with fear, and staying calm may seem like the last thing you can do. But there are a few reasons why it's critical that you try to remain calm during a kidnapping. In a state of panic, your flight-or-fight emotions take over, making it difficult to think clearly or react appropriately. If you panic, you might not pick up on opportunities to escape. And if you are taken, try to turn your focus from your fear to observing as many details as you can about who has abducted you and where they are taking you. Know that focusing on picking up details will also keep your mind engaged, and you'll be less likely to panic.

Know the Two Kinds of Kidnapping

High-Value Target

There are two kinds of kidnapping. In the first kind, you're a high-value target and your kidnappers believe they will receive a large ransom for your return. You might be a high-profile CEO of a big corporation, a high-net-worth individual, or you may be related to a high-net-worth individual. If this is the case, chances are that, while they may injure you, ultimately they want to keep you alive. In situations like these, your kidnappers are likely organized, professional, and have planned out your kidnapping in advance.

Quick Access to Money or Other Goods

In the other kind of kidnapping, you are being snatched solely for access to your bank account or car. It might be an "express kidnapping," where the people who have taken you will have you drain the money in your bank account until it's empty, or they'll demand a ransom from your family. These guys might be lifelong petty criminals or common junkies. They just want your money, and unfortunately there's a chance they're prepared to kill you for it. If you are unable to avoid being taken away by such people, you'll have to proceed very carefully.

TACTIC #2: PARTICIPATE IN YOUR OWN RESCUE

Collect as Many Details as You Can

While you might have just put up the fight of your life, you need to behave in a submissive manner once it's clear you're going to be taken. You don't want to fight at this point and risk further injury. Put your head down and don't look them in the eye. You want to give the idea that you're going to be a good hostage—

quiet and compliant. You want your kidnappers to think you'll do whatever is asked of you. Meanwhile, you need to pay close attention to what's going on. Note as many of the following details as possible:

▶ How are your kidnappers dressed? (If you're not blindfolded.)

▶ How many voices are you hearing?

▶ What language are they speaking? Do you detect any accents?

▶ Are any names being used? Repeated phrases?

In the Transport Vehicle: If You Can, Try to Visualize the Route Being Taken

▶ How many turns?

▶ Can you hear street noise?

▶ How fast are you going?

▶ Are you on a highway or a city street?

▶ How long do you think you've been in the vehicle?

In the Holding Spot or Safe House (You May Be Taken to Several Places)

Once you are brought inside a location, you should notice as much as you can about your surroundings and what's happening there.

▶ Do you hear any sounds from the street?

▶ Are there any noises in the building?

▶ Can you hear if others are being held?

▶ Do you smell anything?

- ▶ If there are no windows, use the change in temperature to determine differences between night and day.
- ▶ What kind of schedule do your captors keep? Are people coming and going at certain times? Are they eating or sleeping at different times of day?

> **The longer you're held captive, the greater the chance you'll get out alive.**

You are in one of the most stressful situations imaginable. Try to remember that by collecting details you are participating in your own rescue. Also know that the longer you're held captive, the greater the chance you'll get out alive.

Leave a DNA Trail

What most Americans don't know is that you can start leaving a DNA trail that could help authorities find you. It doesn't sound pretty—but leaving behind a trail of spit, blood, or even vomit can allow authorities to retrace your steps. The DNA can also be used to positively ID that you are in fact the victim, and sometimes it also creates a time stamp for where you were at a specific time in your capture. Try biting your tongue until it bleeds and then spitting, or pulling out a clump of your hair. Don't make it obvious that you're doing this on purpose. Spit while coughing or crying. If at all possible, leave DNA in each place the attackers take you—including at the scene of the abduction and in any transport vehicles.

Leaving DNA in Safe Houses: What You Need to Know First

Once you are taken to a safe house you'll want to continue to leave a trail of DNA. But most kidnappers are smart enough to wash down surfaces to hide any traces that you've been there. So how do you continue leaving a trail of DNA? In order to leave behind DNA that won't be removed by your kidnappers, two things *must* happen:

1) Have a Conversation About Kidnapping Survival

     You need to discuss this tactic with your loved ones. You need to share what you've learned about leaving DNA behind in the event of a kidnapping. Should your family ever have any reason to believe you have been kidnapped, they should inform the police, and also tell them you've been trained in kidnapping survival tactics. This lets the police know that when they find a location where you have been taken, they can look for your DNA in unusual places. This also puts you, as a victim, in a higher position. You're not a helpless victim, but a trained individual leaving clues to help the authorities find you.

2) Leave DNA in Unusual Places

     You want to keep leaving DNA, but any spit or blood you leave in a safe house is going to be wiped away by your kidnappers. However, they aren't going to clean areas such as under tables, behind furniture, or under rugs. It sounds crazy, but these are the ideal places for you to continue your DNA trail. Leave your hair, fingerprints, or, even better, bloody fingerprints. And because your family has informed the authorities that you're trained in kidnapping survival tactics, they'll know to search in these places for traces that you've been there.

Build a Rapport

If you hear the kidnappers talking about being Muslim, appeal to their religious side by explaining that you believe in God too. Family is a topic that most people have feelings about, so talk about your kids—or about being a brother or sister. You may be able to connect about mundane topics such as hobbies or even sports. The goal is for your kidnapper to view you as a human being—and not an object. Talking with your kidnappers can also help reveal some important information that may help you survive.

GOOD BEHAVIOR MAY CREATE COMPLACENCY

One of the reasons you need to behave in a submissive manner is so that they don't see you as a security risk. If you're yelling and screaming, they might tape your mouth shut. If you're fighting, they might tie you up or chain you to something. If you do exactly what is asked of you, it's possible they'll become complacent, and they may trust you to stay put and will leave you alone. This means they might not even lock the door of the room you're in. This may present an opportunity to escape.

Identify the Weak Link

Not everyone in a group has the same mind-set. There is likely a leader giving orders, and someone who feels bad about what they are doing to you. You need to determine which kidnapper is the most sensitive. There are several ways to do this. You can try to see if one of your captors will agree to tell your family that you're okay. Or you can look one in the eye—one time—and say,

"I'm in a lot of pain from that fall when you guys took me. Would you get me some Tylenol?" and see if he does. If someone apologizes to you after you've been kicked or pushed—that might be your guy. Also, pay attention if anyone seems to be checking on you more often to see that you are okay, or brings you a little bit more food. This is the person who may end up assisting you during the rescue phase. This person might end up helping you physically escape the place you're being held, he might show you how to get to an exit or help you if you're hurt. Try to exploit this person's sensitive side. Try to appeal to him on any level you can. Be grateful for whatever he brings you. Remember, your goal is to let him see that you are a human being.

FAVORITE SPY TRICK: BUSTING FREE WHEN DUCT-TAPED TO A CHAIR

As I mentioned in *Spy Secrets That Can Save Your Life*, breaking out of duct tape is surprisingly easy to do, and it's the most common way a criminal is going to bind your hands, since duct tape is common and cheap. It's also surprisingly easy to escape if you're duct-taped to a chair. All you need to do is lean back as far as you possibly can, and in one swift and fluid motion move your head toward your knees (as if you were assuming the crash position in an airplane). It's possible that you'll have to repeat the movement more than one time before the tape breaks, but it's entirely possible to do.

TACTIC #3: SURVIVE THE RESCUE OPERATION

While you'll obviously want nothing more than to be rescued, you need to know that a rescue operation is highly dangerous. A rescue is usually attempted only once negotiations for ransom have failed. Rescues are as chaotic as, or perhaps more so than, actual abductions, and you are at risk of being mistaken for one of the kidnappers or shot by a stray bullet.

Establish a Health Problem

You can actually plant the seeds for a safer rescue early on in your captivity. Remember that Tylenol I told you to ask for? That's a perfect opportunity to establish a health problem that might end up saving your life. Let your kidnapper know that you think you sustained an injury. Tell them you have a persistent pain in your abdomen, for example. You can say that you really think something was hurt when they kicked you. Persistently develop this problem during your captivity. It's important, though, that you don't go into too much detail, or make up a health problem that is hard to prove you really have. If you tell them you're diabetic and need insulin, it will be very obvious you're lying when you don't go into a diabetic coma.

The Actual Rescue

What most Americans don't know is that the rescue team will set off a series of environmentally appropriate sounds—a car horn, machinery clanking, a dog barking, or even a rooster crowing (animal sounds would be prerecorded) if you are held in a rural area. That series of sounds—whether it's three consecutive sounds, or maybe two short sounds followed by a long one—alerts the rescue team that it's time to break into the facility from all entry points. Obviously, there's no way for you to know what kind of sounds your rescue team will use as a signal before they break entry. However, as a hostage you can make it a point to listen to what kinds of sounds you hear in the environment you're being held in. You may be able to determine what kinds of sounds would be used and be on the alert for them.

When the entry is breached and the rescuers come in, your fake injury comes into play. *Immediately.* You want to use that injury to have a reason to double over, throwing your body onto the floor, *on your back.* This is the safest position for you to be in. On your back with your hands and legs open and visible. This way the rescue team can see you're not holding a gun or another weapon. It's crucial that you stay down, because your rescuers are going to be ready to shoot at any movement that happens above waist height. If all goes as planned, you will be removed from the facility and receive any medical care you require. When you are able to speak and think clearly, the police or FBI will interview you. All of the details you noted during your abduction will be collected, helping to put your kidnappers away for a very long time.

Author's note: To learn the crucial tactics that can help make sure you and your loved ones don't become the victims of a kidnapping, check out our flagship Spy Escape & Evasion course at www.SpySafety.com.

SPY ENCOUNTERS: LINUS
SEARCHING FOR LEGAL TRAVELERS

The truth is, we sometimes want legal travelers as much as narco-terrorists do—but for completely different reasons. A legal traveler, for our purposes, is someone who can travel from a country that we can easily operate in to a hostile foreign country that we can't easily get into. A legal traveler would be able to enter hostile territory, collect secrets, and bring them back to us on more friendly turf. I found my best legal traveler completely by chance. I was working in Paris, and was casing out the city. I decided to get something to eat, and went into a Middle Eastern restaurant. The restaurant was fairly empty. I took a table with a view of the door, and sat down and ordered my food. While I was waiting, an attractive young woman walked by. She was wearing exercise clothes, and had an air of confidence about her. She stopped by and introduced herself as GRETA. She walked into the kitchen, and actually came back with my food. It turns out that she owned the place. We chatted for a while—and I told her about "my business." My cover that time was "travel agent." She told me about her restaurant, and how she loved serving food from her native Iran. I couldn't believe my luck—and I basically told her so. The only difference was that I told her I needed to establish how safe it was for my clients to travel to Iran, and I'd love to hear more from her on that topic. We made a dinner date for the following night when her restaurant was closed. We had a lovely meal, and I was able to see right away that this woman had access. She casually told me stories of different activities her brothers and uncles were involved in back home, and I could see that this information could be very valuable. I had her checked out, and everything she said was true. I was able to develop her fairly quickly, and it wasn't long before she was bringing me back intelligence from Iran. She traveled there several times a year, and each time she brought me valuable information. I found throughout my career that legal travelers are one of the best tools a case officer can have. I was always grateful to GRETA and the work she did for our country.

CHAPTER SEVEN

PROTECTING THE GREATEST MINDS IN THE WORLD FROM HOSTILE FOREIGN COUNTRIES

How to Travel Safely When Others Want to Harm You

THE REQUIREMENT: Locate asset in the host country and protect individual from possible threats from other hostile countries. Determine if individual is open to working directly with the U.S. government. Obtain information on subject's work pertaining to XXXX XXXXXX XXXXX XXXXXXXX.

PARTICIPANTS: C/O Alvin Henry, hereafter referred to as alias OSCAR.

Hugo Thomas, hereafter referred to as alias/krypto EZRA.

Elias Horvath, hereafter referred to as alias/krypto ISAAC.

A DIFFERENT KIND OF ASSET

I've seen just about everything. I've had moments when I've been absolutely terrified, and I've thought to myself, "I never want to do this kind of work again." I would go home to my family and try to convince myself I should stay put. But then I'd get a call about a requirement and I'd be right back at it. There have also been moments when I couldn't believe how blessed I was to do intelligence work. One of the times when I felt really fortunate was when I was protecting "national assets." "Asset" in this case means something different from what you're probably thinking. The kinds of assets I was protecting weren't property or goods, and they weren't military assets like submarines or planes. I was protecting individuals who were so brilliant, their minds so advanced, that they needed the protection of the U.S. government. These people were usually mathematicians or physicists—some of the biggest brains in the entire world. In many cases, they had developed something, or were capable of developing something, that was so valuable that many countries would want it. That meant the asset was in constant danger of being kidnapped by a hostile foreign country. It was my job to make sure that didn't happen.

IS HE LEGIT?

The first time I worked with a national asset I nearly made a big mess of the entire thing. The United States wanted to know if MATHEMATICIAN X was the real deal. While I'm trained in many areas, there's just no way I could verify if someone was an extraordinary math genius worthy of high-level government protection. That's out of my league. It takes one national asset to verify the qualifications of another—very few people are smart enough to do it. So I was set up to escort MATHEMATICIAN Y (who was a national asset himself) to meet MATHEMATICIAN X. Y was going to determine if X was as brilliant as everyone thought. My job was to protect MATHEMATICIAN Y, but also to pay attention to the meeting. I might not have understood all the talk about mathematical formulas, but we don't really want one national asset talking to another potential asset without some supervision.

All I really had to do was get MATHEMATICIAN Y to the meeting place. But MATHEMATICIAN Y is so valued that he doesn't actually go out in public very often. Putting these two guys together, someplace where they could be spotted, was too dangerous. The plan was to fly MATHEMATICIAN Y on a private plane that would land in the middle of an empty field. Then I'd escort Y over to X. That seemed simple enough. We landed, and had a very short window of time for this meeting to happen. My orders were to have MATHEMATICIAN Y back in the air quickly.

We started walking to the meeting, but were stopped by a significant obstacle. There was a big fence right in the middle of the field, blocking the place we needed to get to. I was getting really nervous. I had one job to do and this could mess it all up. The minutes were ticking. I walked up to the fence, pulled on a post, and much to my surprise, I was able to lift it right out of the ground. Y looked at me like I was Hercules. He just couldn't believe it. I didn't tell him the fence was loose. We took our meeting and were back up in the air soon enough. Looking back, that case was a cinch compared to my others.

SPY VS. SPY

DATE, TIME , & PLACE OF CONTACT: École Polytechnique, Paris, France, November XX, XXXX.

PERSONALIA:

NAME/KRYPTO: ISAAC

AGE: 47

HT/WT: 5'9", 186 LB

HAIR: Blond, long

GLASSES: Yes

PERSONALITY/DEMEANOR/ATTRIBUTES: Withdrawn, quiet, shy, socially awkward. Has developed Formula X, determined to be a valuable contribution to mathematics.

NATIONALITY/CITIZENSHIP: XXXXXX, XXXXXX

KNOWN LANGUAGES: Hungarian, English, Romanian, German (some)

FAMILY: Wife XXXX XXXXXX (45), Daughter XXXXX XXXXXX (16), Daughter XXX XXXXXX (14), Son XXXXXX XXXXXX (12)

ADDRESS: XXXX Rue XXXXXXXX, Paris, France

Everyone wanted ISAAC. He was brilliant and had discovered something that could impact the entire world. It was no surprise that many people wanted this information—or even better, they wanted ISAAC to come work for their country. The United States would have been happy to have him. Unlike other countries, we'd just ask him to work for us and respect ISAAC's answer no matter what it was. Some hostile countries would snatch ISAAC the first chance they got. They'd simply kidnap him and smuggle him into a hostile country. He'd never see his family again and they'd never know what happened to him.

The United States got wind of the fact that ISAAC was being

sent to present a paper at a conference. This was big news for two reasons. First, ISAAC's native country was very protective of him and he was not allowed to exit his country. The only reason he was being allowed out was because his native country was proud of his accomplishment. They wanted to make sure the world knew that a scientist from Country X had made this discovery. Second, the conference was taking place in a friendly country. France was a place a U.S. intelligence officer could move around in with relative ease. My job was to make sure that ISAAC was safe. That might sound strange, since he wasn't an American. The U.S. government just knew how dangerous it could be if certain hostile nations had ISAAC in their possession. Naturally, we'd be thrilled if he came to work for the United States, but my number one priority was keeping him out of harm's way. We couldn't let ISAAC get into the wrong hands.

THEY ARE TARGETS AND THEY'RE BEING WATCHED

Here's another thing you need to know about national assets: Sometimes they lose their freedom. This is true to varying degrees for such geniuses all over the world. The truth is, their minds are so valuable that they're going to be watched just in case they are compromised. Is this person traveling anywhere strange? Are they traveling more frequently than usual? (And by the way, in some countries national assets aren't allowed to leave their native country at all, while others may just be prohibited from traveling to certain places.) A national asset's finances are also monitored, since a large influx of cash is a red flag that something is up.

RELATIONSHIPS ARE EVERYTHING

I only had a few days to work, so in addition to securing ISAAC's safety I had to try to develop a rapport with him very quickly. I went to the conference and listened to his lecture, barely understanding a word. At lunchtime, I noticed that several other men seemed to be intensely watching ISAAC. I was able to get confirmation from my colleagues that these guys were in fact from a very hostile country, and they were going to snatch ISAAC the very second they could. It was tempting to approach ISAAC and alert him to the situation, but that could cause a big problem. If the other spies saw me talking to ISAAC, I would be burning myself. It would be obvious that I was an intelligence officer, and I didn't want that to happen. I had to find another way to keep ISAAC away from these seriously bad guys. I had to act quickly, and that's when I had an idea. I saw EZRA standing in the corner of the room. He was one of the people running the conference, and we had enjoyed a nice conversation when I arrived that morning. I made sure to be very warm and friendly, and I let him know how excited I was to be in his country.

BREAKING A RULE TO SAVE A LIFE

I called EZRA over and told him I needed to speak to him immediately in private. EZRA could sense that I was worried. I told him we were going to have a frank discussion, and I needed him to trust me. That's when I broke the rules and I admitted I was at the conference on behalf of the U.S. government. I told him that certain individuals were planning to kidnap ISAAC, and it would be a disaster if that happened. The world would be in danger. It would also look terrible for the host country, and lastly an innocent man would be pulled away from his family.

I knew that if these guys were planning to kidnap ISAAC it meant they had vehicles parked nearby. I had one of my colleagues figure out where the cars were parked, and sure enough, they were right outside. I told EZRA that I needed him to find a way to get the cars towed. Immediately. EZRA was a little confused and surprised, but said he'd do it. Only a few minutes passed, and there was an announcement that certain cars were about to be towed. Sure enough, the guys who I suspected worked for Country X went running out of the building.

I remember almost laughing to myself because these guys were actually wearing trench coats. It was like something right out of a spy novel.

THINK LIKE A SPY: MAKE RELATIONSHIPS EVERYWHERE YOU GO

The idea that spies are always slipping in and out of shadows—never being seen by anyone—is totally wrong. While there are obviously moments when a spy doesn't want to be seen, much of the time a spy knows that making relationships everywhere is crucial to his or her success or even survival. Spies will chat up bellhops, taxi drivers, waiters, maids—anyone who might prove helpful if something happens. All of the people you meet going about your everyday life or while traveling hold different bits of information. You never know when that information might be useful to you, or even when it might save your life.

A RISKY MOVE

I finally met ISAAC, and did my best to convince him to work for the U.S. government. Bottom line, he wasn't interested. But that didn't mean I wasn't going to try to get a copy of what ISAAC discovered.

I knew where ISAAC was staying, and I went over to his hotel while other presentations were being given. I walked through the lobby like I owned the place, and no one questioned me. I went up to the fourth floor and located his room. It was locked, of course. But luckily I saw a maid down the hall. I was determined to get into that room, so I put a big smile on my face and explained to the maid that I really needed to use the bathroom—desperately—but I had forgotten my key and could she help. I even started to squirm like a little kid. She believed me, and let me right into ISAAC's room. ISAAC had made no attempt to hide his items. Right there on a table was a pile of floppy disks, and they were clearly labeled with the name of his presentation. I pocketed them, hoping there would be more valuable information on the disks. I couldn't steal them, though. After the near-kidnapping attempt I knew ISAAC would be on high alert and would report to the police that the disks were missing. I had to get these disks copied and back into his room quickly—he'd never know they were missing. Keep in mind that this was years before personal computers were common, so I had to find a way to get these copied quickly.

THINK LIKE A SPY: ACT LIKE YOU OWN THE PLACE

I'm not suggesting that you do anything illegal like trespassing. However, there are times when you might need access to a restricted area. Maybe you're trying to get away from someone who you think is following you, or maybe there's an emergency taking place and it's the only safe place for you to be. The secret to accessing restricted areas is simple—just act like you're supposed to be there. Don't glance around the area looking to see who's paying attention. Just behave normally, and chances are no one will question you.

EZRA had really impressed me by figuring out how to get the bad guys' cars towed so quickly. He just jumped right on it and made it happen. I implored him again—I reminded him that my presence helped thwart a major kidnapping at his conference, and I needed him to help me *one more time.* He was reluctant, of course, but he did it. He copied the disks for me. I immediately got a copy to the necessary personnel—and then did the more complicated work of breaking back into ISAAC'S hotel room to put his disks back. I wiped up all my fingerprints and made sure there was no sign I was ever there.

A NEW SPY IS BORN

The last part of my operation involved a meeting with intelligence in my host country. The disks were analyzed, and we realized ISAAC had his paper as well as his classified government work on the same disks. This was intelligence *of major significance*. Not only was there information about Formula X (ISAAC's creation), but we now had Country X's entire encryption system. It was a huge coup. I knew that this wouldn't have happened without EZRA. His quick thinking and willingness to help out America was key. I was sure to explain this to the intelligence officers in EZRA's country.

I was satisfied that I had fulfilled my requirement. ISAAC was safe, we had gained major intelligence, and I was still in one piece. Later on, I was very proud to receive some major awards for this operation. It always feels good to be recognized for your work. But it was nothing compared to a surprise I got a few months down the line. I was busy on another operation, in another country, when much to my surprise I ran into EZRA. It turned out, his country was so impressed with his skills that they trained him to be an intelligence officer. Knowing that another spy was born, and that I had something to do with it, was one of the proudest moments of my career.

YOUR INNER SPY

Spies are constantly faced with situations where they have to make split-second decisions. A colleague of mine describes it as like being in the middle of a car wreck—the car is spinning. What do you do? Do you steer or apply the brakes? You have a moment to decide before your car crashes right into the huge semi that's up ahead. In the story you've just heard, OSCAR is faced with a major decision—break the rules and tell EZRA that he needs his help and that he's actually working for the U.S. government, or risk a couple of goons snatching ISAAC on OSCAR's watch. Which is worse? Spies are constantly assessing situations and asking, "What can I do? What are the possibilities? What is the right decision to make with the information I have right now?"

TACTIC #1: ASSESS YOUR OPTIONS—THE OODA LOOP

To help assess situations and enable the best possible decision making, guys like OSCAR use something called the "OODA loop." The OODA loop was created by a former Air Force captain named John Boyd to help pilots make decisions during air combat. However, the OODA loop can help you clarify the decision-making process in many different situations, from how to react in an emergency to making important business decisions. The OODA loop is a four-part decision process that helps intelligence officers make the best decisions possible—and very quickly. The four parts are: observe, orient, decide, and act.

Part One: Observe

In part one, you need to assess the information you currently have and look at information from as many sources as possible. The more information you have available to you, the better the perception you have. Ask yourself the following questions to ensure you're picking up all of the information available to you:

► Are there circumstances unfolding that I need to know about?
► What is happening right now? What direct impact does it have on me?

▶ Is anything happening that can affect me indirectly?

▶ Is there anything happening that might impact things for me at a later time?

▶ Have I made accurate predictions about what's happening?

▶ Is there a big difference between prediction and the reality of what's happening?

Part Two: Orient

The idea with part two is to become more aware of how your perceptions impact your thinking and/or decision making. By having a clearer idea of how *you* perceive things, you can move through the OODA loop process faster. A challenge people face during this stage is that everyone's view of things is influenced by their own life experiences and perceptions. You're also reorienting yourself all the time as new information comes to you via the observation phase. There are five influences that you need to be aware of during this phase of the loop:

▶ Cultural traditions.

▶ Genetic heritage.

▶ The ability to analyze and synthesize information.

▶ Previous experiences.

▶ New information.

Part Three: Decide

This stage is where the actual decision is made, based on your observations and orientation. But any spy will tell you that as new information continues to pour in, your decision-making process can be impacted. Many things will run through your mind, from where will you go to how will you move, when will you move, who you need to avoid, and how you escape. As you learn to move through the cycle, you'll start to see that all the information from part one is filtered through the orientation phase—where your perceptions ultimately help influence the decision you end up making.

Part Four: Act

This is where your decision becomes action. However, it is important to note that the action actually starts the loop all over again. Now you must observe how the action you've taken has changed the situation. You must observe again, orient, decide, and ultimately act based on how the situation is now playing out.

It sounds complicated (especially when we're talking about making life-altering decisions in a matter of seconds), but if you start to practice this cycle you'll see how your mind starts to funnel through this process almost effortlessly. Becoming aware of how you process information can have a huge impact on outcomes—whether you're dealing with a big business decision or an imminent threat.

TACTIC #2: TRAVELING IN THE AGE OF TERRORISM

We've all woken up, turned on the news, and discovered that many lives have been lost in another tragedy such as the terrorist attacks that have taken place in France, Belgium, Turkey, and Germany. Travel has never been more complicated, and at times the idea of leaving home can seem overwhelming or even frightening. It can be tempting to avoid travel, whether it's for business or pleasure. But I believe in empowering yourself so that you can travel with confidence. Intelligence officers are well-prepared travelers—and that's been true long before terrorism became one of the biggest concerns on every American's mind. This is how spies do it.

Build Relationships Everywhere You Go

OSCAR started building a relationship with EZRA the second he arrived at the conference. Obviously, at the time he had no idea that later that day he'd be asking EZRA to call the police and get potential kidnappers' cars towed. But that's why spies are always building relationships. Yes, part of that relationship-building might be related to looking for new sources of information—but it doesn't stop there. Spies will make relationships everywhere they travel, because they never know when one of those casual relationships will end up saving their lives.

SPY ENCOUNTERS WHILE TRAVELING
MAX: A Near-Mugging

I was on an assignment in Paris. I was actually just enjoying a regular dinner out on the town with a friend—I wasn't taking a personal meeting or dining with a potential agent. When I arrived at the restaurant, I was greeted by the maître d'. I did my best to say hello in French and tell him I was looking forward to our dinner. I was kind to everyone, from the busboy to the waiter. I asked lots of questions, but in a friendly way. I also complimented them on the food, which was incredible. My buddy and I were full after we finished our entrées, so we asked for the check and were planning to leave. One of the busboys came over after we asked for the check. He seemed nervous, and he actually told us to stay put, and suggested we have some dessert. I protested at first, but there was something about the way he was talking to us that made me think we should just stay. We ended up having dessert and another drink. On my way out, I discreetly asked the busboy, 'Why did you want us to stay?' His English wasn't great, but I got the gist of what he was saying. 'This area is popular for muggers. They pay some of us to let them know when Americans are leaving the restaurant. I didn't want you to get mugged.' I thanked him, grateful that I had listened—and glad once again that I had been kind to a person who had the ability to keep me out of harm's way.

SAM: A Near-Bombing

I will never forget the time the concierge at the hotel I was staying at suggested I don't go out one night. I had been going out nightly to case the city I was working in. I've found the people at the front desk of a hotel in a foreign country really have their ear to the ground about what's going on, so I'm always especially nice to them. I tip heavily, and always greet them warmly as I come and go from the hotel. The night he told me to stay in? Terrorists bombed a disco frequented by Americans. I can't say that's where I would have been headed, but I appreciated him making the effort to keep me out of harm's way.

As you can see, developing a good rapport with different people when you travel can help ensure your safety—or at the very least make your trip more pleasant. Making a connection with everyone from the concierge and the maid to the waiters and shopkeepers can make a huge difference if you are overseas during an emergency. You never know when they might tip you off—or provide essential information about what to do if there is an emergency.

Be sure to follow these additional spy tips to stay safe when traveling.

Support the Local Economy

That means frequent the same places locals use. Don't stay at a hotel that's full of Americans, and don't eat at touristy restaurants. The truth is, generally speaking, terrorists are less likely to blow up their own people.

Go Deep into the Culture

This is part of casing out a foreign city. Make a connection with the people providing your services. Thank them when appropriate and make conversation about family and children. Tell them how you are enjoying your stay in their country. Research customs before you travel. Do people shake hands or is touching considered inappropriate? Is looking people in the eye important or offensive? Your efforts will always be appreciated—and they might just keep you safe.

Practice What Intelligence Officers Call the "Custom-Made Smile"

During an introduction, when the other person says their name, say it back to them while giving them a big but sincere smile. Subconsciously this makes a positive impact on the person you are meeting, and fosters an immediate sense of trust.

WHEN YOU SHOULD AVOID AMERICAN EMBASSIES

I recommend finding out where the U.S. embassy or consulate is located before you travel outside the United States. Unexpected things may happen—passports get lost or stolen, or someone becomes seriously ill—and the embassy can be a big help. However, there are times when you should avoid the embassy. If you are abroad and a major terrorist attack happens—especially one that is perpetrated against Westerners—I would not recommend going to the embassy. If Westerners are the target, it's entirely possible the area immediately around certain embassies will become dangerous. In that case, I would recommend staying in areas that are less likely to be populated by Westerners until the immediate crisis is over.

Spy Travel Essentials

In *Spy Secrets That Can Save Your Life* I discussed some basic travel safety rules—such as which seats you should never book on a plane, and how to stay safe in a taxi. Now I'm going to share some higher-level safety tactics that intelligence officers always follow. It is my hope that you won't let fear stop you from traveling for work or while taking your family on wonderful vacations. I do hope you'll make a point to be careful, and will ensure the safety of yourself and your family, by taking the following measures.

The Travel-Ready Kit: What to Take with You

Unfortunately, terrorism is a major concern today. However, there are a few inexpensive items you can easily pack that might save your life. These items would also prove invaluable if you were ever caught in a big fire in a hotel.

Flashlight: A simple item that you might not think to take on a vacation. If the lights go out during a fire, or while you're in a crowded train station, you'll be able to see where you are going and where the exits are located. This can mean the difference between life and death. To get a FREE flashlight, the flashlight I take with me when I travel, visit www.SpyFlashlight.com.

A P100 Mask: In the event of a chemical attack, this mask can actually filter out much of the harmful chemicals, as well as ash, dust, and other toxins that will be floating around in the air. These masks can be found for under $10. I recommend getting the ones that have an air vent. If you are running, not having a vent may encumber your breathing and make it harder for you to get away. Have a mask for each member of your family.

Safety Goggles: In a major disaster, such as when the Twin Towers fell on 9/11, the smoke and dust are so thick that people are forced to close their eyes while making their escape. Keeping a simple pair of safety goggles handy will enable you to keep your eyes open, making it easier for you to escape to safety.

A Rigger's Belt, Paracord (About Twenty Feet), and a Carabiner: A rigger's belt looks much like an ordinary belt. The only difference is it can hold five thousand pounds. You could use this belt and your paracord to lower your family members to safety in the event of a fire or explosion. Paracord can also be used to tie your children's hands to yours, connecting them to you should you have to escape.

Cheap, Brightly Colored Rain Ponchos: Not only will these be handy if it's pouring rain while you're traveling, but a bright yellow or bright orange rain poncho can be an excellent way to keep track of your family in an emergency. You can all identify each other by the bright color, making it easier to stick together or locate one another if you are separated.

A Multitool: Useful for cutting something open, cutting paracord, and much more.

Antibiotics: I believe you should take a supply of antibiotics with you. In the event of an extreme emergency situation it may be impossible to get access to this infection-fighting medicine.

FAVORITE SPY TOOL:
THE BEST HOTEL HIDING PLACES

I certainly hope you would never hide your cash or other valuables under the hotel mattress or in the toilet tank. That's the first place a criminal is going to look. If you absolutely have to hide something in your hotel room, there are two places I recommend.

THE BATHTUB SPOUT: Simply stick the item you want to hide up the bathtub spout, and then pack it with toilet paper so it doesn't fall out. If you do this, be sure to use the "Do Not Disturb" sign on your door so that housekeeping doesn't stumble upon your stash while cleaning.

THE SHOWER CURTAIN ROD: This takes a bit more time and energy, but it's a good hiding place. Use your multitool to pry off one of the ends of the curtain rod, and stash your cash or valuables in the tube.

To see more places you can hide your valuables in hotels and in your own home, be sure to visit www.SurviveLikeaSpy.com for a free training video I put together for you.

SPY ENCOUNTERS: CORMAC
PENETRATING THE CIRCLE

Sometimes there are groups you just can't break into—no matter what. In these situations you have to find someone who is so appealing to whoever your target is that they won't be able to resist. They'll let the guy into their circle, thinking they've won a great prize—but in reality, this person is collecting secrets and sending them back to you.

This is a situation I've seen many times over the course of my career. Take Iran, for example. You just can't approach an Iranian professor or researcher hoping you'll be able to work him and eventually get him to tell you secrets about the nuclear program. It's impossible. In a situation like that, you have to use a penetration agent. It's the same process of spotting, assessing, and developing, but the only difference is that in this case you're finding someone else who can penetrate the circle. I had six different aliases, and I might come off as a friendly Scot at a state dinner to someone I'd started a dossier on. I'm interested in this guy because he's hanging out with people who have access to information we want. He doesn't have the information—but he associates with people who do.

I might start talking to him about how our countries need to know each other better, maybe keeping the talk on just economics. I wouldn't bring up anything nuclear. I'd get him comfortable discussing his political views. I find something he can easily get for me. It's like a side job: He gets me something and I get him a bit of money. A way down the line, once he's used to the clandestine nature of the relationship, the requirements start getting harder—but he gets more in return. Eventually he's a full-fledged agent. He's penetrated the circle for me, getting info from people I can't get to. He's not giving me secrets of his own, but the secrets of his associates, friends, or coworkers.

CHAPTER EIGHT

TURNING A SOLDIER INTO A SPY

How a First-Time Case Officer Taught a Decorated War Hero to Do Brush Passes, Dead Drops, and Signaling to Help the United States

THE REQUIREMENT: Find individual to transplant into hostile territory in North Vietnam. Once this individual is settled in the North, assist them in establishing a clandestine operation that will enable them to organize, collect, and communicate intelligence to U.S. intelligence officers.

PARTICIPANTS: C/O Henry Frazier, hereafter referred to as alias CORMAC.

Trang Ngu, hereafter referred to as alias/krypto REX.

MY FIRST AGENT

I've never forgotten REX. He was the first agent I had ever worked with as a case officer, and it proved to be a very challenging operation. REX was a highly decorated war hero who had been wounded several times in battle. But even more extraordinary than that, he was willing to do something really big for the U.S. government. Another case officer had found

REX and, before handing him off to me, discovered REX was willing to "defect." What that really meant was that he was going to let us make him "disappear." He'd get taken out of Cambodia by a body smuggler, only to eventually pop up at the North Vietnamese embassy saying he wanted to defect. A war hero from the other side would be impossible to resist. Someone like REX, who was in the military, would have lots of information and valuable secrets. It seemed very likely that they'd allow him to defect. Once REX got settled, we'd set him up with everything he needed to funnel secrets back to us. That was the plan anyway.

A CROOKED BODY SMUGGLER

Unfortunately for REX, the first time we tried to make him disappear was a complete disaster. We had to make everything look as real as possible, so that meant REX had to be taken out of the country by a real smuggler. The U.S. government couldn't get him out with someone pretending to be a smuggler. If they got caught, or the Vietnamese government decided to do some digging, they needed to immediately discover that this smuggler was a really bad guy. The situation needed to look legitimate. So REX worked the black market to find a body smuggler to take him out of South Vietnam and across the border into Cambodia. REX's next move after that would be to go into North Vietnam, approach the embassy, and ask for asylum. The whole thing was a mess. The body smuggler took his money and deserted him and left him alone in the jungle—with nothing. REX was tough and incredibly determined, though. He managed to walk all the way right back through the jungle. He communicated to his case officer shortly after he got back that he hadn't made it.

At that point, the United States decided it would be a good idea to give REX some extra training before he attempted to defect again, and that's when he was handed over to me.

TRAINING REX

DATE, TIME, & PLACE OF CONTACT: Safe House, April XXXX, LOCATION STILL CLASSIFIED.

PERSONALIA:

NAME/KRYPTO: REX

AGE: 26

HT/WT: 5'5", 152 LB

HAIR: Short, military-style

GLASSES: No

PERSONALITY/DEMEANOR/ATTRIBUTES: Highly adaptive, skilled, quick-thinking. Shows dedication and determination. Has undergone discrimination and shows great interest in helping U.S. interests. Wounded several times, recovered well.

NATIONALITY/CITIZENSHIP: Vietnamese-Chinese, Vietnamese

KNOWN LANGUAGES: Vietnamese, Chinese, English

FAMILY: Mother XXXX XX (51), Father XXXXX XX (55), Brother XXX XX (16), Brother XX XXXX (15)

ADDRESS: Army barracks

REX and I were set up in a safe house together, and the idea was that I'd spend the next three months training him. We'd work on some basic tradecraft, as well as encryption and decryption skills. One of the most important jobs a case officer has is to protect his assets, so we take the training of agents very seriously. Until you actually do it, many people can't conceptualize a brush pass, a dead drop, or how to use signals or a concealment device. These moves might sound easy, but then you see someone try to execute them, and it's a big mess. You have to work closely with an agent, and figure out what works best when it comes to communicating and passing information along to that person. Training REX went well—he was smart and eager—but I faced some unusual challenges that had nothing to do with the tradecraft training itself.

REX was supposed to stay in the safe house, completely out of sight. Obviously, we didn't want him to be seen with me. But apparently being cooped up all the time was too much for him, because eventually I realized that he was slipping out and even managing to find girlfriends. This made me really nervous, for obvious reasons. It was my first case and I didn't want to screw up, but I figured I couldn't really keep this guy a prisoner for the next three months. I ended up agreeing to drive him around—I even dropped him off places and took him out for dinner once in a while. I thought his chances of not being caught might be better if I stuck around to keep an eye on him. He was always wearing civilian clothes, so that helped. I also made sure to take him out only after dark, and to choose places I thought we would be relatively safe. Luckily, we never got caught.

WHAT IS A SAFE HOUSE REALLY LIKE?

There are many different kinds of safe houses all over the world. They range from a random, generic hotel room used as a temporary safe house, to a regular suburban home. Some safe houses have what is known as a "safe house keeper." This would be an ordinary civilian with a highly unusual job. It might be a young man—a bachelor, who goes off to work every day like most people. But he has a very interesting side job: He's also keeping the house stocked and prepared for any operatives who may need to come in and out. He may also pick up operatives from the airport. Chances are, the neighbors wouldn't even notice. It would appear that he's a regular person who occasionally has overnight guests.

Sometimes, especially in war zones, military bases are used as temporary safe houses. Some operatives carry an ID that allows them on any U.S. military base in the world. However, most intelligence officers will tell you that you should never bring a sensitive asset on an American base because you can't let them be seen. The asset must remain a secret, even from other individuals on a base. In certain parts of the world, that could cause problems—like the individual being executed. When dealing with a sensitive asset, it's better to transfer them to a warehouse or another safe site.

THE WRONG GUY, AND LEARNING A BIG LESSON

I had a really embarrassing incident one night when I was picking up REX. It was such a rookie mistake, but I also learned how important it is to be careful when picking up your agent—or the guy you *think* is your agent. I wanted REX to blend in, so he purposely dressed like everyone else around him. It was a poorer, more rural area, so he wore simple clothes. Unfortunately for me, REX might have blended in a little too well. I was driving my car down a quiet dirt road in the early evening. I had arranged with REX previously that I'd pick him up along the road at a certain time. I could see REX a couple of hundred yards ahead of me. He was wearing short pants, a button-down shirt, and thongs. I slowed the car down, and REX didn't turn around—I assumed he knew it was me in the car. What I usually did was slow the car way down, and REX would quickly hop into the backseat. We had done this many times before and I barely even had to stop. REX got in, and I started talking to him. He didn't say anything back, which was unusual. I turned around, and immediately realized I'd made a huge mistake. I didn't pick up REX. I picked up a completely different person. Just as I was realizing my mistake, this guy was seeing he'd made a mistake too. It immediately became obvious to me that he was an agent too, just as he was seeing that I wasn't his case officer. He got out of the car, and I drove off to find REX—which I eventually did. I had no choice but to look at the bright side. I might have messed up, but now I knew the person I picked up was working for someone else—and not necessarily for the U.S. government. I'd have to keep my eye out for him from now on.

THINK LIKE A SPY: BE PREPARED TO BE FLEXIBLE WHEN IT REALLY MATTERS

Obviously it would have been bad if REX were spotted. However, it was clear to CORMAC that, while REX was an excellent agent and was picking up what he was being taught very quickly, the problem with this guy was that he wasn't going to stay put. REX had no interest in staying inside a house for three months. Rather than force the issue, CORMAC decided that he would try to control the situation to the best of his ability by taking REX out himself. It might not have been ideal, but he could manage where and when REX was going out. Had CORMAC instead insisted on strictly enforcing the rules, REX probably would have gone out anyway—but on his own he was much more likely to get caught, which would have ruined their operation. Don't sabotage a situation because you refuse to be flexible.

CLANDESTINE COMMUNICATIONS

REX was an excellent student and learned quickly. The first thing I trained him to do was use the microdot reader, which was a small piece of Plexiglas about half an inch long that works much like a magnifying glass. A microdot camera would capture the text of the message we wanted to send and shrink it all down to something approximately the size of a period. Any regular-looking piece of correspondence could actually contain a secret message in the form of a microdot, legible only to those with access to a reader.

We also worked with the "one-time pad," or OTP, which is another means of using a secret code to communicate. Both the agent and the case officer would get a copy of the OTP, with one person taking the pad for encoding, the other the pad for decoding. The text is paired with secret random keys that are listed in five-digit groupings. Sheets from one-time pads were never used twice (hence the name), making them nearly impossible to crack. After a sheet was used, it would be destroyed. Once REX mastered these different means of covert communication, I taught him how to use a one-way voice link, or OWVL. This meant that he could tune in to a certain frequency on the shortwave radio and wait to hear a specific five-digit number that was meant as a signal to him. Following his signal code would be the real message REX needed to hear (encrypted, of course). He would then write down the numbers, and decode the message using a miniaturized codebook.

SMUGGLING REX AND THE EQUIPMENT

DATE, TIME, & PLACE OF CONTACT: Safe house, August XXXX, LOCATION STILL CLASSIFIED.

When we felt that REX was ready to try being smuggled over the border again, we realized we had an additional obstacle to tackle. Now that REX was trained in covert communication skills, we wanted him to have access to a microdot reader, codebooks, and a shortwave radio. Obviously, REX couldn't be smuggled into a hostile country carrying any of those things. He wouldn't have anything other than the clothes on his back and some food. All of his supplies would have to be brought to him covertly. And this was where our problem came in. We could find a way to get the stuff he needed across the border covertly, but we would need a way to communicate to REX that the items were ready to be picked up. After much planning and some genius work by the technical team, we were able to provide REX with a simple pair of thongs that had a secret compartment. It was just big enough to hold a microdot reader and a miniature codebook. Now we had a way to keep in touch with REX, and to tell him when the other supplies he needed were ready to be picked up.

A SNAFU THAT COST US EVERYTHING

REX was told to contact a smuggler again, and we all prayed that this time it would go as it should. This time the plan was for REX to be smuggled into Phnom Penh, the capital of Cambodia. Once he got there he would find the Hong Kong accommodation address. A dead drop had also been loaded with some crucial items—some much-needed cash, and the first message that he would decipher with his microdot reader.

After REX "disappeared," it took quite some time for him to be listed as a deserter. When it finally happened this news proved incredibly difficult for his family. They knew nothing about what REX was doing, and it was shameful to them that he was a deserter.

I was waiting anxiously for a communication. I was in a difficult position, because North Vietnam was a denied area for the United States. We had no embassy in North Vietnam, nor any secure facilities. The only help we would have was from an asset in the Hong Kong office. I breathed a big sigh of relief when we received word that REX had made it across safely. REX arrived intact even though he was once again robbed by the smugglers. After decrypting his first microdot message, he knew that he was supposed to head to a library in Phnom Penh. There was a dead drop waiting for him, hidden carefully below a shelf of books in the history section. He let us know he had unloaded the dead drop and received a package by inserting a thumbtack on the wall near the bathroom for our asset to see. It seemed like everything was off to a great start.

The next order of business was for REX to purchase a shortwave radio so that we could continue communicating with him. He did this, and transmitted a message saying that he was safe and was going to scout out the North Vietnamese embassy tomorrow. The next day REX arrived at the embassy. He was received by a senior army captain and explained that he wanted to defect. REX was interrogated for two harrowing hours, and eventually told to come back in two weeks after they conducted an investigation. Two weeks were going to feel like a long time, but I was confident that REX's story would check out fine. REX was a decorated war hero, and that was documented in newspapers. His story could easily be checked out and verified.

We all anxiously waited out the next couple of weeks until REX's next appointment at the embassy. When he got there, REX was told they were not yet finished conducting the investigation. This of course started to make everyone nervous. It was clear that REX was being strung along, and I didn't want him to end up in jail. I was frantically trying to get my chief of operations to do something, but I was left frustrated. I was even told, "Spending a night or two in jail would be good for his story." I wasn't getting anywhere, and I was worried for REX's safety. Unfortunately, this situation got even worse. I soon received a message that said something to this effect:

WHERE ARE YOU, WHY ARE YOU IGNORING ME? WHY HAVE YOU DESERTED ME? I NEED MONEY, AND THIS IS A VERY BAD SITU-ATION. I'M GOING TO SELL MY RADIO, MICRODOT READER, AND OTPS. I HAVE NO CHOICE. PLEASE RESPOND.

The captain in North Vietnam continued to drag out the situation and there was nothing I could do. It soon became clear that there was a snafu, and it was causing a serious problem. I had been sending REX covert messages via the shortwave radio, but it was obvious he wasn't receiving them. It soon became clear that REX had confused the time difference, and was listening for our signals at the wrong time. REX was patiently listening to the radio, hoping to hear the signal and receive a message from us, but he was never going to hear our message and any further communication was impossible. His last message stated something along the lines of that he was going to try to make it to the Viet Cong on his own. But he never made it. Shortly after we received this communication from REX there were massive B-52 strikes along the Ho Chi Minh Trail. We had to assume that REX was killed. This story ended tragically. A year later he was presumed dead. There was no way he could have survived. His family never knew what he did—even though a courier brought them $10,000 in cash. They never knew what happened to him, or about the heroic actions he took. He died with his family thinking he had defected.

THINK LIKE A SPY: PAY ATTENTION TO EVERY DETAIL

In this case, a major mistake was made that could have been easily avoided—and the consequences were deadly. Unfortunately, it's not uncommon for people to make plans, only to have them be messed up when we fail to take into account a simple but crucial detail like a time difference. Double-check details when making plans to avoid mistakes that can cost you frustration, time, money, or life.

YOUR INNER SPY

Technology has obviously changed dramatically since the days of the Cold War, providing intelligence agents with newer and more sophisticated ways of gathering intelligence. However, any spy will tell you that no technology can beat the information you can collect with clandestine HUMINT, aka tradecraft. This means that intelligence officers still have to be highly skilled at tradecraft. Passing off and receiving actual information from other people still is and will always be a critical part of an intelligence officer's job. These tactics aren't difficult to master with practice, they're fun too, and we practice these skills and many others at our Ultimate Spy Week, www.UltimateSpyWeek.com.

TACTIC #1: CLANDESTINE HUMINT OPERATIONAL TECHNIQUES

Brush Passes

When a spy needs to physically pass an item to another operative, they'll do a brush pass. When it's done right, no one will see that a physical item has changed hands—onlookers will just see you brush past each other in a casual way, without noticing that you've actually swapped identical-looking items. Chances are you're not going to be in a situation where you have to slip something to someone without being detected, but brush passes are fun to do and easy to practice. To do it successfully, it's best to be in a crowded area, where people walking around will make it hard for you to be seen passing the object. You would predetermine with the other operative what kind of object you'll both be holding. They need to appear identical. You could use a magazine, a newspaper, a briefcase, or even an umbrella. You would store the note or object you want the other person to get within the item that's being passed. Once the operatives have spotted each other, they'd quickly exchange items. As they each walk their own way, it looks like they still have the original item in their hands.

Dead Drops and Concealment Devices

When a case officer like CORMAC needs to get information or supplies to an agent like REX, they'll do a dead drop. A dead drop is a standard way of passing something along to another person covertly. While a simple object like a newspaper works perfectly for a brush pass, a concealment device is needed for a dead drop. Throughout history, some surprising and clever items have been used as concealment devices. Secret messages have been encased in wine corks and coins. Information has been stuffed into teeth. And believe it or not, at one time it wasn't uncommon to use dead animals as concealment devices. Once intelligence officers figured out that dousing the dead animal with a bit of hot sauce kept other animals away, secret items were stuffed into the carcass and then sewn up. While such objects are interesting, you'll be relieved to know that something as simple as a small box will work just fine. Just keep the following in mind when preparing a concealment device for a dead drop:

- ▶ While your object needs to be identifiable by the person who is picking it up, you also want to make sure it blends in with the environment. Don't use something that's odd or interesting enough that someone else will be tempted to pick it up.
- ▶ While you are "hiding" your concealment device, remember that while you are hiding it in plain sight, your agent needs to be able to locate it without arousing suspicion. While it shouldn't be visible from the street, you also don't want to hide it so well that the other person will be digging around for a long period of time. That will draw attention to the situation.
- ▶ Know the culture of the area and how it might impact your dead drop. If you're in an area where streets are cleaned regularly, think carefully about where you are placing your item. Spies who have worked extensively in Japan know that it is an incredibly clean place. Any concealment device disguised as trash would likely be picked up.

DEAD DROPS: DON'T MAKE THESE MISTAKES

DON'T LOOK BACK

You should know that this is one rookie mistake that can really mess up your dead drop. Once you've made the dead drop, keep moving forward and do not look back. It's human nature to want to leave the item and then turn around to see if anyone is watching you. However, that move is a dead giveaway that you're up to no good, and ultimately you're drawing attention to the item you're leaving behind.

DON'T MAKE IT TOO GOOD

RON needed to pass along some information to another operative. He enclosed the information in a plastic bag and placed it under a rock near a predetermined location by a river. A few days went by, and it became clear that the individual who was supposed to unload the dead drop never did it. RON went back to the location to see what happened, and that's when he realized he'd made a big mistake. It turns out it had rained, and there was mud everywhere, lots of puddles, and all of the rocks had shifted. Even he couldn't find the rock where he left the dead drop. RON learned how badly weather can mess up a dead drop, and he was sure never to make that mistake again.

FAVORITE SPY TOOL: THE CORNCOB CONCEALMENT DEVICE

Believe it or not, my favorite spy tool was inspired by a memory of going to state fairs when I was young. People would get corn on the cob, eat it, and sometimes wouldn't bother to throw the cobs in the garbage. They'd just toss them on the ground. Many years later, when I was working as an intelligence officer in a foreign country, I was walking down the street and I actually encountered a tortoise nibbling on a discarded corncob. He ate it much like a person would, eating any of the corn that was left but not eating the cob itself. I realized that in the country I was currently in (much like back at the state fair) people would throw corncobs on the ground, and it wasn't unusual to see one. I started to think this would make the perfect concealment device. It wouldn't seem unusual, and no one would want to touch it. If an agent knew where to look, he could easily pick it up and access the secret materials inside. It became my favorite concealment device of all time.

Of course, there were parts of the world were my corncob wouldn't work as well—it wouldn't fit in with the environment. In those cases, I've used things like empty energy drink containers, cigarette packages, false bricks, and even emptied-out ChapStick tubes. It's funny, I've really developed a habit—I can't even walk through a parking lot without looking at a stray piece of trash and wondering if that empty soda can is really holding secret information. Probably not, but I can't help it. It's just long years of training kicking in.

TACTIC #2: MOVING DEAD DROPS

The Car Toss

A car toss can be an excellent way to pass along information—it's kind of like a dead drop in motion. There are a few ways a car toss can be approached. One is for the person in the car to slow down, tossing an object outside of the window for the other person to retrieve. A colleague of mine loves to use a sock to stash the secret items he's going to toss. You can spin a sock (like you're about to throw a lasso) and toss it with some velocity if necessary. Conversely, an agent can toss something into a car as it's moving. Obviously, this has to be done with care, as you don't want it to be obvious that something is being thrown to or from the car. It's also possible to stick a concealment device on the car for the other person to retrieve later when the car is parked. It's also possible to throw an item while you're walking (which is called a foot toss). Just keep it simple and remain casual.

After executing a car toss or foot toss, always conduct a surveillance detection route to make sure you aren't being followed. (I've put together a special training video for you where you can see many dead drops in action. You can watch it for free at www.SurviveLikeaSpy.com.)

TACTIC #3: I *THINK* I'VE SEEN HIM BEFORE—HOW TO RECOGNIZE PEOPLE

Being able to recognize people in different environments is a very important skill for a spy to have, and it's also incredibly difficult to master (especially as we saw in CORMAC's account of mistakenly picking up the wrong agent at a meeting point). Many intelligence officers will admit that recognizing faces is something they consistently struggle with and must continue to practice. We've all been in a situation at the store, your kid's school, or church where someone approaches you in a friendly manner and says hello—and you have no idea who the person is. That's awkward, but at least it's not putting you in a dangerous situation. Being able to recognize people in your immediate environment can help you determine if you might be in danger from someone who is following you. One of the best ways to train your brain to recognize people is to practice.

1) Start noticing the people around you when you're out in public. Do they have any distinctive facial features? What does their hair look like? How tall are they and what kind of build do they have?

2) What are they wearing? Are they carrying anything? As I said in *Spy Secrets That Can Change Your Life*, always notice the shoes. Often someone will shed a jacket, put on glasses or a hat, maybe even a wig, but they'll often neglect to change their shoes. So make a point of noticing if they're wearing boots or shoes, sneakers or loafers.

3) What kind of gait do they have? Do they have a long stride? Do they take short steps? Do they move their arms in a particular way when they walk?

4) Are they participating in any memorable behaviors? For example, are they smoking? If they are, try noticing what kind of cigarettes. Or maybe this person is smoking a pipe. Perhaps they are walking a dog. Note anything that might help you remember that person.

5) Who does this person resemble? Sometimes it can help to associate a person with a celebrity they look like. Perhaps someone looks like Clint Eastwood or reminds you of Jack Nicholson. What about them causes you to note that resemblance?

Once you've gotten in the habit of noticing such characteristics, challenge yourself. Pick a person you see out in public and describe him to yourself. Wait an hour or two, and then write down the description. How much can you remember? Continue practicing until noticing a person's characteristics becomes second nature. You just might need it someday.

CHAPTER NINE

GIVING A HIGH-LEVEL AMBASSADOR A BUGGED PAINTING

How to Embed Cameras and Microphones When It's *You* Who Needs to Spy on Someone

THE REQUIREMENT: Find the means to collect intelligence from Vietnam's ambassador to France to aid the United States in ongoing peace talks.

PARTICIPANTS: C/O Daniel Novack, hereafter referred to as alias MARCUS.

Access Agent Pierre Perdue, hereafter referred to as alias MONTE.

TARGET: Don Bach, hereafter referred to as alias/krypto VADIM.

I met MONTE not long after I arrived in France, and he had all the qualities a case officer looks for in an access agent. MONTE was smart, charming, and highly educated, and he and his wife loved to entertain in their palatial apartment. Even better, MONTE was incredibly well connected and part of a very powerful social circle. Everyone loved to attend his cocktail parties, because you never knew who you might run into. There were professors, artists, actresses, musicians, wealthy businessmen, and—luckily for me—ambassadors and other high-level government people. When you're a case officer, you're always looking for someone who has *access*, and MONTE had access to nearly everyone. It took a long time to develop him; MONTE didn't need the money like other people I had worked with. Over time, though, I learned that MONTE agreed with the United States on certain issues. It was that mutual philosophy that eventually got MONTE working for me as an access agent. I also think he found the idea of spying very exciting, which most people do. I really enjoyed working with MONTE because he was clever and quick. We tried some crazy things while we were working together, and let's just say some of them worked out better than others.

THE ART-LOVING DIPLOMAT

DATE, TIME, & PLACE OF CONTACT: September 15, 19XX, 9 p.m., Home of MONTE, CLASSIFIED LOCATION.

My requirement was to collect intelligence from a diplomat who represented the interests of the North Vietnamese government. Big peace talks were happening, and it was my job to get any information I could that would help the United States. I didn't always know exactly what my plan would be to fulfill a requirement, and this was one of those times. After months of watching the diplomat and the people who worked in his house, I had come to the conclusion that I wasn't going to be able to get any of his staff to help me out. They were too loyal. I had to find another way in, and I never imagined that MONTE would come up with a great idea at one of his infamous parties about how to bug an embassy.

MONTE had hosted a dinner party one night, and after dessert guests were hanging around in the living room and on the veranda drinking wine and chatting. MONTE realized he hadn't seen VADIM in a while—he wasn't with any of the groups in the living room or outside. VADIM was a diplomat from North Vietnam, and he was someone MONTE paid much attention to. Getting information from VADIM could be the key to fulfilling our requirement, but we still hadn't figured out how to do it. MONTE had picked up some good bits and pieces of information from cocktail chatter, but nothing that could really help the United States with the peace talks. We needed something much bigger.

MONTE saw that the door to his library was open and there was a light on. He walked in, and found VADIM standing in front of the large painting that was hanging behind MONTE's desk. VADIM was so transfixed by the work of art that he didn't even notice that MONTE had entered the room. After a few moments went by, MONTE said something so that VADIM wouldn't be surprised by his appearance. "It's a beautiful piece of art, isn't it? My wife gave it to me as an anniversary gift and it's one of my most cherished pieces. It was actually painted by an artist in the South of France." MONTE was always a quick thinker. The truth was, it wasn't a gift at all. His wife was from an old French family, and this painting had been in her family for several generations. Much to his wife's chagrin, MONTE didn't even like it all that much. But it was clear that VADIM *did*. They spent the next half an hour talking about the painting's various characteristics—the brushstrokes and the artist's use of lighting. And that's when MONTE got the idea that he should present VADIM with a gift.

BEWARE OF GREEKS BEARING GIFTS

We all know to "beware of Greeks bearing gifts"—and that things didn't end well for the Greeks after they accepted the "gift" of a wooden horse left outside of their city gates. They pulled the massive horse inside, only to later find out it was filled with Trojan warriors ready for a fight. While the gift MONTE had in mind wasn't quite so dramatic, using a "Trojan horse" as a listening device is always very risky. Intelligence officers can use a Trojan horse in the form of a gift, but it's not something that can be taken lightly. The gift might appear to be just an ordinary sculpture, pen, or vase—but inside are listening devices so that every conversation that takes place can be recorded and listened to. The problem is that if the recipient discovers the bug, they know exactly who is responsible, and obviously that creates a really big mess. And in certain countries it's enough to get someone killed.

THE GREAT SEAL BUG

One of the most famous Trojan horses was given to U.S. Ambassador W. Averell Harriman in August 1945. The Vladimir Lenin All-Union Pioneer Organization (a kids' organization not unlike the Boy and Girl Scouts in America) gave the ambassador a hand-carved replica of the Great Seal of the United States as a gift. This gift was hung in the residence of the ambassador, in a place that was absolutely perfect for picking up conversations. What no one knew was that the seal contained one of the first concealed listening devices. Inside the seal was a high-frequency radio bug—that meant it didn't require an outside power source, but was activated by a radio signal from outside the building. In the 1950s, some British radio operators reported hearing a British attaché speaking while listening to Russian radio traffic, and that was deemed very suspicious. Even with this tip, no bug could be found inside the embassy. The device wasn't actually discovered until three ambassadors and many overheard conversations later.

A PAINTING WITH UNIQUE PROPERTIES

The gift that MONTE had in mind was a painting. Since the ambassador loved the painting so much, we decided to have a replica created for him. However, this painting would have a little something extra—a covert listening device. We worked with technical services, who assigned one of their highly skilled artists to create a beautiful replica of MONTE's painting. Nothing about the painting looked out of the ordinary. The canvas and the frame looked normal, and if you picked it up it didn't seem unusually heavy. However, embedded inside the lining of the canvas were a microphone, a transmitter, and a battery powerful enough to run for two years. While we were excited to give this to the ambassador, we were also nervous. Anytime a Trojan horse is used in an operation you have to carefully weigh the risks vs. the rewards. If the listening device is discovered, MONTE would be in big trouble. While he wouldn't be killed in the country we were working in, he would be exposed and would lose all his access. Treason was also a very big concern. We had decided early on that in this case it was worth it. MONTE had worked very hard to develop a relationship with VADIM, and VADIM had no reason to suspect that MONTE would try to bug his house. He planned to give the gift as soon as it was ready.

THINK LIKE A SPY:
WEIGH YOUR RISKS AND REWARDS

There's no point in taking a risk just for risk's sake. Giving the ambassador a bugged painting was incredibly dangerous, and there could be major consequences. However, after the risk and the reward were carefully considered, it was decided that it was not very likely the bug would be found, and that the amount of intelligence that could be gathered was very great. Compare the risks to the rewards before going forward with decisions that could have unwelcome or even dire consequences.

HANGING THE PAINTING

DATE, TIME, & PLACE OF CONTACT: October 12, 19XX, 7 p.m., Home of VADIM, CLASSIFIED LOCATION.

MONTE went to VADIM's beautiful town house to present him with the painting. MONTE told him that he truly appreciated VADIM's friendship, and was deeply moved by his appreciation for art. VADIM was of course delighted with the gift, and accepted it graciously. What VADIM didn't know was that I was sitting in a car right outside with one of my colleagues. We were thrilled to discover that the listening device worked perfectly. We could hear everything they were saying as if we were in the exact same room. VADIM had some high-level people over for dinner that night, and we got a few good tidbits of intelligence. I couldn't believe how brilliantly the painting was going to work out.

The next morning I was back outside the ambassador's town house, eagerly listening for more information. The painting was still sitting in the foyer, not yet hung up. I heard VADIM ask one of his maids a few questions, and then I heard him speaking to another man. The nature of the conversation made it sound like he had a close friend or family member staying over. Whoever this guy was, he also loved the painting. In fact, he thought it was so wonderful that it should be hung in "a place of great honor." VADIM immediately agreed. Those were the last words we heard from VADIM's house. He had decided that the place of honor was on a wall at the top of the stairs—a place where no one in the house ever seemed to have a conversation. I sat outside for a few weeks just to make sure, but it became clear we weren't going to hear any secrets from that beautiful painting after all.

THINK LIKE A SPY:
YOU CAN'T CONTROL EVERYTHING

The biggest concern for MARCUS and MONTE was obviously getting caught. They didn't want MONTE to get burned if someone found out they had bugged the ambassador's house. There was another concern, though: that the ambassador would choose to put the painting someplace where it wouldn't do anyone any good (and that's exactly what happened). Much time and effort is put into creating devices like VADIM's painting, even though everyone involved knows it's entirely possible it won't work out in the end. Spies simply can't control every element of their environment. If you decide not to put effort into something just because it might not work, you might ultimately end up missing out on some good opportunities. It's often worth a shot.

FAVORITE SPY TOOL: THE MULTIPLE PLUG ADAPTER AUDIO DEVICE

One of my favorite tools was a simple everyday device you'd use in any house when you just want to plug a few things into the same outlet. They are something everyone uses, and no one has any reason to suspect they'd be anything but what they are. Except my multiple plug adapter contained a high-powered audio recording device. Like anything else, you can have a great success with one of these—or it can turn out to be a big flop. Once I had a guy infiltrate a film crew who was going to interview a very important figure at his home overseas. As he was "setting up the audio equipment" he casually inserted the multiplug into the outlet and purposefully left it behind. I was excited about what we were going to hear. We got some great information during the first few months and it appeared to be a great success. But then all of a sudden we heard nothing but loud static from time to time. It turned out that the maid had unplugged the vacuum, but she left the multiplug attached to the cord of the vacuum cleaner. The potential for intelligence was so good that we kept listening for a while—but all we'd hear was the regular sound of a maid vacuuming. It was good while it lasted.

SMUGGLING IN A SHORTWAVE RADIO RIGHT UNDER SOMEONE'S NOSE

PARTICIPANTS: C/O Daniel Novack, hereafter referred to as alias MARCUS.

Agent Kwasi Okar, hereafter referred to as alias LINDEN.

I learned very quickly as a case officer that you had to get very creative when it comes to concealing audio devices. You always had to ask yourself, "What might work? What can we conceal something in?" After months of development, I had recruited a third-country diplomat from Africa who was living in North Korea. We were putting him in as a press secretary—some kind of made-up job that wouldn't fall under suspicion. But communicating with him was going to be difficult. Mail couldn't be used at all, because we knew that everything would be read and censored. I needed to get him set up with a shortwave radio, but getting it to him would be nearly impossible. Security was incredibly tight, and anything this man would be bringing with him would be carefully inspected.

THE LUMBER SHORTAGE THAT SPARKED AN IDEA

I started to notice that when various officials moved into the area, it was normal for all of their belongings to come packed in wooden crates. It was also normal to keep the crates around after they was unpacked, because lumber was very scarce. I wondered if technical services could find a way to build a crate that could somehow conceal an entire communications system—everything someone would need to run a shortwave radio. Once again, the technical services guys came through. They managed to create modified four-by-fours that could open up and house the different components of a shortwave radio. Once the wood was reglued and reassembled you couldn't tell it was anything but a regular crate. It didn't even feel heavier than a normal crate. The real test came when it was time for LINDEN to unpack. The security people arrived at LINDEN's house and carefully inspected every single item in the crate. Furniture was inspected for hidden items. Anything that could hide anything was opened up. LINDEN reported that it was a nerve-wracking process that took a very long time. Finally, the security people were satisfied that nothing had been smuggled in. When the crates were empty, LINDEN explained he wanted to keep the lumber and dragged the crates into the backyard. Once he got settled, LINDEN carefully set up the equipment. It worked perfectly, and we got excellent intelligence from LINDEN for several years. This was yet another example of how creativity plays such an important role in intelligence work. You can never stop thinking about new ways to solve problems.

> You can never stop thinking about new ways to solve problems.

YOUR INNER SPY

Staying Safe When You Are Alone

I realize it's unlikely you'll ever find yourself in a situation where you need to forge a painting to bug an embassy. However, there are many instances where embedded cameras and microphones can keep you safe. For example, at Spy Escape & Evasion we teach many Realtors how they can use audio and video equipment to stay safe at work, to avoid horrifying situations like the one Beverly Carter found herself in.

When Arron Lewis, thirty-three, was asked by reporters why he killed forty-nine-year-old real estate agent Beverly Carter, his answer was chilling:

> "She was a rich broker. Because she was just a woman who worked alone—a rich broker."

Carter's body was later found in a shallow grave approximately twenty miles northeast of Little Rock, Arkansas. Carter had called her husband to let him know that she was showing a property at five-thirty, and let him know where the house was. Three hours passed, and when he didn't hear from his wife, Carl Carter felt strongly that something was wrong and decided to go out to the property. When he arrived, the door to the home was open, her car was in the driveway, and her purse and wallet were still inside. He entered the home, but found no trace of his wife. He later received text messages saying, "My battery is low" and "I'm out drinking with friends." But Beverly Carter didn't drink. Her husband feared the worst, and unfortunately he was right. Tragically, Beverly Carter was found dead near the concrete company where the killer worked. Carter's death caused tremendous fear within the community of real estate agents, who often work alone and with total strangers.

When Your Loved Ones Are Alone

In New York City, a babysitter was accused of abusing a six-month-old baby who was in her care. The family had installed cameras and witnessed the babysitter "appearing to grab the child out of the crib and throw the child down." In California, a mother viewed her nanny-cam footage to find what appeared to be her babysitter smothering her thirteen-month-old-son to quiet his crying. Thankfully, neither child was seriously injured. Young children aren't the only ones who are at risk. In Queens, New York, camera footage showed a home health care aide abusing an elderly stroke victim. The aide was seen slapping him and trying to force-feed him.

These are obviously worst-case scenarios, and I hope you never find yourself in any of these situations. If you are concerned about staying safe while working alone, there are many safety measures you can take to protect yourself. If you want to make sure that a loved one is being well cared for, or that your personal property is safe, there are many forms of technology you can easily use to monitor what's happening in your home.

TACTIC #1: USING A CAMERA

Cameras and audio equipment can be used to monitor the behavior of people caring for kids or the elderly, and can let you know with certainty if the people you have working inside or around your home (cleaners, contractors, gardeners, landscapers, dog sitters, repairmen, etc.) are as honest as you hope they are. Cameras can give you peace of mind. Any parent knows how difficult it is to use a new babysitter—even when that babysitter comes highly recommended and has provided excellent references. Being in the position of caring for an elderly or sick parent is also difficult. You naturally want to make sure they are receiving the best care possible. And of course we want to make sure our valuables are safe from anyone who has access to our homes. Today there are more options than ever before when it comes to using a camera. To ensure that you are using a camera properly, be sure to do the following.

Know the Law

In some states you cannot record audio of someone without the knowledge and consent of the person being recorded. This is why some video security cameras capture visual images only. Research what is allowed in your state before installing cameras. I've suggested to the Realtors I work with who are concerned about their own safety as well as the property in the homes they are showing that they simply have their clients sign in, and on the sign-in sheet it says, "To protect the homeowners, there are cameras placed throughout the house." It would also work to hang a sign in the entryway warning individuals that cameras are being used throughout the house.

Find the Right Camera for You

Cameras can be put in nearly anything today. I've seen cameras used in Kleenex boxes, clocks, teddy bears, and picture frames. There are also many different services that enable you to use your smartphone to monitor what's going on in your home when you're away. In fact, one of my colleagues was recently on a plane, in midair, when the woman next to him was able to see via her smartphone that she was receiving a package at her front door. Research the options available and decide what suits your purposes best.

Know What's Legal in Your State

Whenever installing video or audio equipment—even in your own home—take the time to find out what's legal in your state. Know if you can videotape someone in your home without their consent, and be aware of areas that are likely off-limits, like bathrooms and bedrooms.

Review the Footage on a Regular Basis

None of the footage you're taking will do you any good if you don't actually watch it on a regular basis. You'd be surprised how many people go to the trouble of installing cameras, and then never watch what they've recorded. Pick a regular time when it's convenient to review the footage, and make a habit of doing it consistently.

Listen to Your Gut

I'm not suggesting you suspect ill of everyone who comes into your home. However, trust your gut. If you're reviewing the camera footage, and you see nothing wrong but still *feel* like something is wrong, take other measures. Talk to the person about what's going on, or start coming home at irregular times to see what's actually happening. If you do not feel comfortable with someone who has access to your home, ultimately you should obviously not have him or her there, even if you don't have concrete evidence of wrongdoing.

TACTIC #2: ENSURING YOUR PERSONAL SAFETY WHEN WORKING ALONE

As I mentioned, I've had the opportunity to work with many business owners, especially real estate agents, who are concerned for their safety, and for good reason. It's essentially real estate agents' job to walk into private property with strangers, and sometimes they are even expected to drive them around in their own personal car. As we saw with the Beverly Carter story, being a real estate agent can actually be incredibly dangerous. Of course, real estate isn't the only profession that puts an individual in danger. Kala Brown from South Carolina was answering a cleaning ad with her boyfriend when she found herself in a horrifying situation. The individual who had placed the ad was actually a convicted sex offender. He allegedly shot and killed Kala's boyfriend right in front of her, and then kept Kala chained by the neck in a metal container for two months before she was rescued. There are many service-driven or client-driven jobs that require a person to enter a home of someone they do not know—home health aides, nurses, insurance agents, child-care providers (that includes young people who might be babysitting to earn some extra money), tutors, occupational therapists, contractors, electricians, plumbers, cleaners, and so forth. It's important that you always practice the following safety measures:

- ▶ Whenever possible when starting a new position, meet the individual you'll be working for in a public place first.
- ▶ Ask to see identification.
- ▶ Always let someone know where you are going and when you expect to be back.
- ▶ Keep your phone charged and within reach. If you ever feel uncomfortable, leave the house and call for help. You can also say something like, "I've just heard from

my business partner, and they are on their way over to check up on me." Then it will appear you will not be alone in the house for long.

▶ Protect your personal information. You do not need to give out your home address or home telephone number.

▶ Don't get in the car with someone you don't know. Nor should you agree to drive another person somewhere in your own personal vehicle.

▶ Watch where you park your car. Don't park in a place where your car could be blocked later by another vehicle. You want to be able to get out quickly if you need to.

▶ Always have a self-defense tool on your person to protect yourself. The number one tool that I carry, and so do my family members and clients, is the Tactical Pen. You can see videos and details of this pen at www .TacticalSpyPen.com.

SPY ENCOUNTERS: MAX
RETIRING AN AGENT

We all talk about what it's like to spot a source, develop a rapport with someone, and ultimately recruit him as an agent. It's exciting, and it's something most case officers will admit they enjoy doing. What we talk about much less is what it's like to "retire" an agent. It's really difficult, and can be painful for both parties. I also think it's true that any case officer who is good at what he does genuinely cares for his agents—and that's what makes it so hard. A kinship has been developed, and then one day you have to say, "I'm sorry, we don't need you anymore." The money they've gotten used to getting dries up, the excitement of gathering intelligence is over—there's no longer a need for signaling or dead drops. And even worse, the relationship is terminated.

Relationships with agents have to be terminated for many reasons—and it's never easy. I had to terminate a relationship with a legal traveler who was consistently bringing me good information—her expectations of the relationship were becoming unmanageable. Sometimes it's simply that you're moving on to a new country, and you need to turn over your agent to a new case officer. That doesn't always feel good for the agent—they feel like they are being tossed aside. The worst thing, though, is when something tragic happens to an agent. Luckily it's not something I experienced often. But I will never forget talking on the radio to an agent of mine who was in distress. He believed someone was about to come after him. Before I could formulate a plan to help him, I heard his door being broken down, and the sound of gunshots. That was one of the most difficult moments of my entire career.

CHAPTER TEN

THE SPY WHO SOLD CHINA COMPUTERS SECRETLY INFECTED WITH MALWARE

How CIA Officers Avoid Being Hacked, Spied On, or Scammed

THE REQUIREMENT: Create a method to monitor communications in China to gather any intelligence regarding possible developments that would impact the United States' relations with China.

PARTICIPANTS: C/O Marshall Mueller, hereafter referred to as alias WYATT.

Henry Wang, hereafter referred to as alias JASPER.

TARGET: Da Lee, hereafter referred to as alias/krypto SILAS.

PERSONALIA:

NAME/KRYPTO: SILAS

AGE: 29

HT/WT: 5'7", 161 LB

HAIR: Black, short, thin, straight

GLASSES: Yes

PERSONALITY/DEMEANOR/ATTRIBUTES: Smart, sharp, hard-working, sense that he is overwhelmed by duties at his job. Hangs out with friends after work.

NATIONALITY/CITIZENSHIP: Chinese

KNOWN LANGUAGES: Chinese, English

PROCLIVITIES: Spends time with friends, they attend rugby matches regularly, plays badminton. Has spoken to friends about desire to visit the United States of America. Would like to get married soon.

FAMILY: None

ADDRESS: XXXXX, XXXXXXX, XXXXX, Hong Kong

TELEPHONE NUMBER: XXX-XXX–XXXX

THE SMALL AGENCY WITH BIG ACCESS

I heard of SILAS from a contact I had at a local university. SILAS did well in his computer science classes at his university, he was smart, but, unlike some of his classmates, his skills weren't going to help him land a big job at a tech company—or even better, a job that would take him to Silicon Valley in the United States. However, he did get a job working for a small government agency—one that just happened to communicate frequently with many other parts of the government. SILAS's agency had access to other, bigger parts of the government. At that time, due to the export control board, it was difficult for the Chinese to get access to the technology they needed. The good news was that this provided a very big in for the U.S. government.

The contact we had at the university, JASPER, was an agent for the United States, and he kept in touch with SILAS.

We weren't initially sure that SILAS would be useful, but when he started working for a government agency I asked JASPER to keep tabs on him. So SILAS and JASPER met for tea or dinner on a regular basis. SILAS seemed to enjoy having his former professor's advice and attention. There were many areas of his new job that he found challenging, and he was always happy to have JASPER's perspective. SILAS was thrilled to have a steady job, but it wasn't flashy or glamorous like the jobs that some of his classmates had landed. SILAS wanted to excel at work as quickly as possible, ideally moving on to a job that paid better and had more cachet.

Computers That Come with an Added Bonus (for the United States, Anyway)

Over tea one evening, SILAS expressed how much easier his job would be if he could get his hands on more computers. His team could get work done much faster, and more efficiently, and that would reflect well on him. But because he worked for a relatively small office, getting more computers wasn't considered a priority. This gave JASPER an idea, and he signaled me so that I knew he would like to talk the next day. We met around lunchtime, and he told me about SILAS's desire for more computers. Could this actually be the access point we were looking for? I got in touch with my people back home, and we started to explore how we might use this opportunity to get intelligence for the U.S. government. It was decided that we were going to arrange for SILAS to get his computers, but they were going to come loaded with a little more than he might have bargained for.

THINK LIKE A SPY: SOMETIMES A SIMPLE WAY IS A BETTER WAY

SILAS was not a high-level government employee. He worked for a small government agency, and didn't have a particularly important role. However, JASPER and WYATT saw a big opportunity here. They understood that SILAS presented a way in to the Chinese government that wouldn't likely be heavily looked at by anyone who might get suspicious. They didn't dismiss him and try to find a bigger fish. They examined the opportunity, saw how it could lead to big things, and made it work. Don't dismiss an opportunity because it might seem too simple or too small.

> Don't dismiss an opportunity because it might seem too simple or too small.

THE TECHNOLOGY COMPANY THAT NEVER REALLY EXISTED

Just a couple of weeks later, I had my first meeting with SILAS. He was excited to meet me, since his professor had told him I could be helpful. This was one of those instances when I was very happy to have an introduction. In certain countries, meeting a person via another respected person can get you very far. Because I was connected to JASPER, SILAS was very comfortable and open when we met. I had set up a fake company called XXXXXX and had business cards, brochures, everything I needed to seem legit. There was nothing to indicate that I didn't really work at a tech company—we had covered all of our bases—and even if there was, SILAS was so eager to get his hands on more computers that it was entirely possible he would have overlooked it.

I gave him a spiel about how I could get computers to him because of a special arrangement my company had with his country. We talked about what he needed and wanted, and I told him that I could make it happen. What he didn't know was that all sorts of strings were being pulled and arrangements being made so we could just get the computers to his office without raising a massive amount of suspicion. While that was taking place, my colleagues back home were busy adding a little something extra into the computers.

THINK LIKE A SPY: THE POWER OF SHOKAI

We all know connections matter, and that's no different in the espionage game. Sometimes the best way to get a person to trust you is by asking someone to give you a personal introduction. This is especially true in countries like Japan, where shokai, or personal introduction, goes a long way. WYATT was able to make a quick connection with SILAS because he allowed JASPER to make the introduction. Often asking someone else to take the time to make a personal introduction will get you further in a shorter amount of time.

THE ONE TIME YOU CAN'T "BEAT IT TO FIT AND PAINT IT TO MATCH"

If the goal of the United States is to monitor what's going on in another country's cyber infrastructure, we have to be very precise. There's no figuring out how to solve a problem last-minute—or flying by the seat of our pants—ever. Things have to be done quickly, but they also have to be done right. Our plan was to build "back doors" into the computers we were going to get to SILAS. The computers would have Trojan horses and malware built into the system—and done in a way so that even if they literally scrubbed the entire hard drive, it would still be there. The system was designed so that it would sleep for thirty days—maybe more—and then activate. This would enable our people to see everything that was going on and to monitor who was doing what. We also set things up so that these guys would think they were getting valuable information from us that they weren't supposed to have. Of course, this was done on purpose, and we could see how they would respond or react to this incorrect (but very salacious and secret) information. This operation could not have gone any smoother. The United States got a lot of good intelligence—and even better, SILAS never had any idea.

SPY ENCOUNTERS: SAM
HOW A COMPUTER HACK CAN PROTECT A DANGEROUS MISSION—OR DESTROY IT

When you're a pilot protecting the United States, you understand that you might have to risk your life flying through certain hostile airspaces. It's part of the job. Fortunately, our government has figured out some measures to get us in and out of hostile airspace quickly, and hopefully without being shot at. As part of our preparations for this type of mission, our guys would use "meaconing." They would carefully hack into the hostile country's computer system. The result would be that the hostile country's air control would receive a legitimate-looking message saying that they should expect some "routine maintenance" with the system, resulting in a brief shutdown of communication. During this incredibly short period of time that the "maintenance" was taking place, we'd fly through the hostile airspace, picking up as much information as we possibly could—and getting out before we could be detected or anyone could figure out that the United States was using meaconing to get somewhere we weren't supposed to be. In those cases, meaconing was a great help. However, it's also something we are trained to watch out for, because meaconing can be used against us too. It's possible that one of our enemies could try to trick us. They could intercept our signals, or rebroadcast our signals in a way that would tell us to fly off our original flight path. In that situation, we could be lured directly into enemy territory, where they're ready for us—just waiting to shoot us down.

YOUR INNER SPY

It seems like a week doesn't go by when there isn't news of a major hacking—and it's often at places where the average American frequently finds themselves putting down a credit card. In 2014, Home Depot announced fifty-six million credit cards were compromised. After Target stores were hacked, between one and three million of the forty million stolen cards were sold on the black market. It's not just retailers, either—Equifax, Gmail, and Yahoo have both reported major hacks. When so much of our work, household expenses, bill paying, banking, investing, and communication are done online, how can you make sure your information is safe?

WHY I DON'T BRING MY COMPUTER INTO THE BEDROOM—AND YOU SHOULDN'T EITHER

If you could see me sitting at my computer right now, you'd notice I have a small piece of masking tape covering the camera. Getting a piece of tape takes just seconds, and can ensure that you don't have a terrible experience like Cassidy Wolf. Cassidy, who had been crowned Miss Teen USA, had a terrible ordeal involving her computer's webcam. One day Wolf received an email that had three attachments. The email told her that a hacker had nude images of her and he threatened to make them public. Wolf shared her story with Anderson Cooper, telling him, "My mom and I were in tears and in shock. We couldn't believe this could really happen. Your bedroom is your most private and intimate space. To think that someone was watching me in my bedroom for a year and had all my most intimate moments, he had conversations I had with my mom and my brother, and knew everything about my life—someone can have access to all of that by your computer." It turns out that Wolf was being watched by a former classmate who was a computer science major—and Wolf is not alone. A half million people have been victims of "creepware." No doubt it's likely this number will continue to climb. At the rate technology grows, there are going to be more programs and more ways for criminals to hack people's webcams and other computer devices. So play it safe: cover your computer camera with masking tape, and urge your family members to do the same. And lastly, don't bring your computer or device with you anyplace where you wouldn't want to be seen.

YOUR COMPUTER IS AN ENTRY POINT INTO YOUR LIFE

In the old days, things were different. People called each other on landlines, and sent letters through what's now fondly referred to as snail mail. But now, if you're like most Americans, your computer is something you use just about every day (and quite possibly all day long). Even if you're not on a computer at work, you're on your personal laptop, smartphone, or tablet. Because computers play such a crucial role in our day-to-day lives and our dependence on technology is growing, it's important that you know how to use these devices safely. Sometimes all it takes is giving one person the wrong piece of information, and it's like you've given them the keys to your belongings. Your credit cards can be used, checks written on your account, and your most personal information given out. By no means am I suggesting that you stop shopping online or stop paying your bills online— technology can be wonderful and can make life much easier. Just make sure you're protecting all of your vital information.

IT ALL STARTS WITH YOUR PASSWORDS

I know we have a million things to remember to do every day—and having different passwords for different accounts, or changing the ones you already have memorized, might sound overwhelming. It's easy to think it's something you can put off. But ask anyone who has been hacked how difficult, time-consuming, and potentially costly it is to deal with the hacking, and they'll probably tell you they wished they had taken more precautions. Taking some basic measures to protect your information today can keep your personal information safe from hackers.

TAKE THE TIME TO CHANGE YOUR PASSWORDS REGULARLY: We've all heard this advice countless times by now, yet many people don't follow it. If you make a habit of changing your passwords on a regular basis this will become routine. Until you have become accustomed to changing your passwords, mark your calendar or set an alarm on your phone reminding you to do this. It's a simple thing to do and it can save you some major headaches. For instance, to keep things very simple, change your passwords at the beginning of each month.

BE AWARE OF PASSWORD ENTROPY: Password entropy is a measure of how predictable a password is and how hard it would be for a criminal to crack. Password entropy is related to the characters used, as well as the length. A password is much harder to break when a combination of lowercase, uppercase, numbers, and symbols are used. The more complex your entropy is, the smaller the space there is for a hacker to break in. However, your password is useless if you can't remember it. While it's great to protect yourself by coming up with a complicated password, it doesn't do you any good if you can't remember it. You need to find a balance between complicated and memorable.

EVERY PASSWORD SHOULD MEET THE FOLLOW-ING BASIC CRITERIA: A password should have an absolute minimum of twelve to fourteen characters. You should always use a mix of numbers, symbols, and upper- and lowercase letters. Don't use obvious substitutions for letters. For example, you aren't really fooling anyone if you replace an "O" with a zero.

DON'T USE THE SAME PASSWORD: Another piece of information you already know is that you shouldn't use the same password for your different accounts—and again, this is advice many people don't follow, with sometimes devastating results. The bottom line is that if a hacker gets hold of just one password, they can now get into all of your accounts—including your bank account. Keep in mind that some companies and institutions have better security systems than others, and hopefully that includes your bank. So while it might not be easy for a hacker to get into your life savings, it might be a piece of cake for him to hack into the site where you just used the same password to send your aunt an e-card on her birthday. Now a criminal has access to all of your accounts that use the same password, including your bank.

DON'T OVERTHINK IT: I'm sure you know to avoid cliché (and very risky) passwords such as your kids' names, your spouse's name, your pet's name, etc. If you struggle to come up with new ideas for passwords, try the following: Just decide on a random word—anything that pops into your head. Anything. Mix up all the letters, and replace letters with numbers and punctuation marks. For example, from where I'm writing I see a water bottle and a flashlight. Either of these can become the basis for passwords.

Don't overthink it, just go with something ordinary that you can easily transform into a more complicated password.

JUST WRITE IT DOWN AND STICK IT IN AN UN-LIKELY PLACE: If you're changing your passwords regularly and are concerned about remembering them, consider writing them down on a Post-it and keeping it in a place that only you will be able to find—such as inside a favorite book or in a fireproof safe that's well hidden in your home. Let's face it, a criminal isn't likely to ransack your home looking for a small piece of paper with your password written on it. That being said, I certainly wouldn't tempt fate by keeping it near your computer, in your wallet, or in an obvious place on your desk or in your office.

USE MULTIFACTOR AUTHORIZATION: While this adds an extra step to the log-in process, it's safer and can save you much trouble in the end. After you log in with your password, they'll send you a message with a code. (This will usually be a text message but it doesn't have to be.) You must enter the one-time code you receive in order to go any further. Many popular sites offer this, including Google, Twitter, and Facebook.

SECURITY QUESTIONS ARE A JOKE: "What is your mother's maiden name?" or "Where did you go to grade school?" This isn't exactly a high-level security tactic, and if someone is smart enough (and determined enough) to hack your account, they could certainly manage to find the answers to these questions. Sure, it's an extra deterrent, but security questions are not something you can count on to keep your information safe. You can also answer security questions with an additional password instead of your mother's actual maiden name or the name of your school. That means even more passwords to keep track of, but more levels of security too.

ALWAYS CHANGE YOUR PASSWORDS IF THERE IS ANY SUSPICION WHATSOEVER THAT AN ACCOUNT HAS BEEN COMPROMISED.

DON'T EMAIL ANYTHING THAT CAN'T BE ON THE FRONT PAGE OF TOMORROW'S NEWSPAPER: I agree with everyone who says, "If you wouldn't want to see it published on the front page of the *New York Times*, then don't email it." Email was never meant to be secure—it wasn't designed with privacy or security in mind. Incredibly sensitive information—your Social Security number, bank information, tax returns, and confidential business correspondence—shouldn't be sent via email unless it's encrypted.

> **Email was never meant to be secure.**

USING THE INTERNET IN PUBLIC: WHAT YOU NEED TO KNOW

Life isn't as simple as it used to be. We're not going to the office in the morning, grinding out eight hours of work, and heading home with all of our work done for the day. Let's face it, many of us are working hard and taking advantage of those extra moments when you can slip in some extra work. This means we're often working at coffee shops, in waiting rooms, at airports, and even on airplanes. We're hopping online every chance we get. This might be good when it comes to getting work done—but there are risks involved. Hackers love it when people use public Wi-Fi, because public Wi-Fi is an open connection that is usually unencrypted and unsecured. This means you can end up being the victim of a "man-in-the-middle attack." A man-in-the-middle attack occurs when a criminal sees a security flaw and uses it to intercept data from a network. In this instance, a hacker can see any information that you use on the websites you're going to. A hacker can see account log-ins, passwords, and purchases.

PASSWORDS FOR PUBLIC WI-FI DO NOT SOLVE THE PROBLEM

You're working at a local coffee shop and you want to get online. You see a sign that says to ask the barista for the password. You go up to the counter, and after she finishes making someone's cup of coffee she hands you a card with the password printed on it. That is not any safer than public Wi-Fi that does not require a password. If everyone has access to the password, it's just as public and the same security concerns are still there. All a hacker has to do is ask the barista for the same password she just gave you.

THE DANGEROUS ROGUE HOT SPOT

If you open up your computer and there's a free, open connection, don't use it. What you might be seeing is a "rogue hot spot." A rogue hot spot is a free connection that might have a very similar name to a legitimate hot spot. A criminal will set this up to trick people into using his network. Once you connect to a rogue hot spot, a hacker can steal your data and also infect you with malware. Malware is short for "malicious software." Like the name suggests, malware is a program or file that is meant to harm your computer. The malware could introduce a virus, worm, Trojan horse, or spyware. Malware can do anything from steal data, delete data, encrypt data, or even hijack your computer functions.

HOW TO AVOID GETTING HACKED WHILE USING PUBLIC WI-FI

To stay completely safe, you'd avoid all public Wi-Fi connections completely—but I realize that's not realistic. The good news is that there are a few easy things you can do to decrease your chances of getting hacked while using the Internet out in public.

Use a VPN: Start Today

Sign up for a VPN, or virtual private network service. What this does is add a wall between you and the Internet by routing everything in an encrypted format through an actual server that is controlled by your VPN service provider. If a hacker is watching what you're doing, they're not going to see anything. All they'll see is a bunch of nonsense because everything you're doing is encrypted. There are various services you can choose from, and they are affordable. Using a VPN is a must for anyone who uses a public Wi-Fi to do work, and I never surf public Wi-Fi without using my VPN.

Update Your Software on a Regular Basis

We've all turned on our computers and have gotten a message that tells us it's time to update our software. If you're like most people, you click "ignore" and figure you can do it another day. If you're using public Wi-Fi, keeping your software up-to-date is another defense mechanism against hackers. Sometimes updates are designed to fix bugs that compromise encryption. If you're software isn't up-to-date, you're leaving the door open just a bit for a criminal to walk in.

Don't Get Scammed

In *Spy Secrets That Can Save Your Life* I talked about how criminals use social engineering tactics to scam innocent Americans. The Internet is obviously an easy place for criminals to target people. The stories and scams just keep growing. Even CIA Director John Brennan was the victim of a scam—by a teenager. The hacker Justin Liverman, aka D3F4ULT, told *Wired* magazine that he and two other people did a reverse lookup of John Brennan's mobile phone number to see what service he used. When they found out he was a Verizon customer, Liverman called Verizon posing as a technician who couldn't access a customer's database on his own because his "tools were down." Verizon asked for a "V-code," which is just a four-digit number assigned to each employee. Liverman made one up on the spot, and it worked. Liverman was able to get Brennan's account number, his PIN number, is AOL email address, and the last four digits of his bank card number. Liverman and his colleagues didn't stop there. They called AOL and said they were locked out of their account. What was the security question they needed to answer? "What are the last four digits on the bank card?" They had already gotten that information from Verizon, so they were able to get AOL to reset the password. They were then able to read Brennan's email, which held classified information he had emailed from his work account. They were able to see attachments that contained the names and Social Security numbers of some U.S. intelligence officers, a letter from the Senate asking the CIA to stop using interrogation tactics, and other sensitive materials. Screenshots of some of these materials were tweeted by the hackers. This embarrassing breach just goes to show that it's incredibly easy to get someone's personal information, and that you have to take serious precautions.

Delete, Don't Click

An associate of mine decided to do a little experiment. He sent an email to 250 people with a subject line that read as follows:

THIS IS A VIRUS

But he didn't stop there. The attachment that was sent along with it actually was an Excel spreadsheet that was labeled, *in flashing letters*:

MACROVIRUS

You'd think that would be enough to stop people, but it wasn't. He was shocked to discover that not only did people open the email, some of them actually opened the file that was clearly labeled and literally flashing the word "MACROVIRUS."

PHISHING AND SPEARPHISHING: WHAT YOU NEED TO KNOW

We've all received suspicious emails—some of them might be from someone we know, but the subject says something strange, or just has a link. Chances are that by now many of you have received the "I have millions of dollars but I'm overseas and need your help" email. There are countless varieties of this scam. Delete, don't open.

PHISHING VS. SPEARPHISHING

Phishing is when someone attempts to get your private information by sending emails that appear to be from credible sources—a bank, the federal government, a business you've worked with. Some people will even create a fake website that looks legit, hoping you'll fall for it. Once you respond to their request, they'll ask you for personal information such as a Social Security number, bank account number, or password. Your information will then be used to commit fraud. Phishing schemes are generally directed toward a large group of people (thus they're named after a "fishing expedition"), as the criminal knows that chances are someone is likely to answer and give him the information he wants.

Spearphishing is a personal attack. This kind of attack will appear to come from a site or business you are familiar with, and you know they already have some of your personal information. This takes more work and planning. Because this kind of attack is tailored specifically to you, it can be harder to recognize.

BASIC RULES TO AVOID ATTACKS

PRACTICE SKEPTICISM: Don't simply open every email you receive. If something seems off to you, do not open it. Delete the email. Also, do not click on links sent from places that appear real just because you know you do business with them (such as your bank). And keep in mind: the IRS never emails anyone.

Also, know that just because the email already contains your personal information, such as your phone number, address, or even Social Security number, that doesn't mean it is legitimate. Someone may have searched out that information in an effort to trick you more easily.

PUT YOUR MOUSE ON THE LINK: If you hover your cursor over the link, the real URL will be revealed. This is a simple way to see if an email is legit. If it's different from what the email says, it's fake. It is also true that many phishing sites don't even bother to create real-looking URLs, so the real URL might not even be close to what the link says. Get in the habit of checking URLs before opening an email or clicking on links in the email.

DON'T MAKE THINGS EASIER BY REGISTERING YOUR INFORMATION: When buying things online, there's always an option to register your information to make shopping easier next time. What you're really doing is making things easier for criminals if the site is hacked. Skip this step and instead check out as a guest. The few extra moments spent could save you a lot of trouble in the long run.

THINGS YOU SHOULD NEVER DO IF YOU WANT TO KEEP YOUR INFORMATION SECURE AND PRIVATE

▶ Never share a computer account.
▶ Never use the same password for more than one account.
▶ Never give out your password to anyone—this includes people who claim to be from customer service or security.
▶ Never communicate a password by phone, email, or instant message.
▶ Never leave a computer unattended if you haven't logged off.
▶ Never have the same password for applications and operating systems.
▶ Never use a password that doesn't contain letters, numbers, and symbols.

CHAPTER ELEVEN

TAKING CONTROL

What You Can Do Right Now to Lead a Secure Life and Survive Anything from Blackouts to Economic Collapses to Home Invasions

You've just heard some exciting stories from some of the most highly trained intelligence officers in the field. The stories shared in this book demonstrated how spy skills and quick thinking got intelligence officers out of many dangerous situations. All of the tactics you've just read about aren't just for intelligence officers working operations out in the field—they're for you too. Life can be unpredictable. And while it's always my hope you aren't faced with the challenges that come along with a natural disaster, a criminal act, or any sort of catastrophe, I believe in being prepared. I also believe in being self-reliant. It simply isn't safe to put yourself in a position to depend on other people to help you or your loved ones should disaster strike. While I don't think you should live in fear, believing the worst could happen at any time, the simple fact is there are specific steps you can take right now to give yourself the peace of mind that you're living as safely as possible. I'm committed to finding new ways to help you and your family live safer, happier, and more successful lives, and I'm about to share some additional, potentially life-saving skills with you.

TACTIC #1: WATER PREPAREDNESS

Water Emergencies Are Dangerous: Always Be Prepared

Society can quickly break down if water is not available. Unfortunately, there have been many instances where people have suffered or died needlessly because they could not gain access to water. ISIS has used water as a weapon in recent years, with devastating results. They have cut off the water supply to villages to assert their rule. When residents of some villages had to flee, only to return when their village was finally unoccupied again, they had to leave again, discovering their village no longer had a supply of water. Tragically, people were left suffering and dying of thirst. According to the *Washington Post*, "Children and older people are succumbing in the 100-plus degree heat. There is no place to bury them on the rocky hill. The Iraqi government has tried to drop water to them, with little success. There are children dying on the mountain, on the roads. There is no water, there is no vegetation, and they are completely cut off and surrounded by Islamic State. It's a disaster, a total disaster."

In West Virginia, toxic chemicals used to process coal were spilled into the Elk River, making the water supply unsafe, and many residents were not prepared. Schools and businesses had to close, bottled water was quickly sold out at stores, and people waited in long lines to get water from the National Guard. One concerned mother told the *Huffington Post*, "I went from feeling happy anticipation for what the New Year held to being filled with uncertainty and fear for our family's health. Being afraid that you are not keeping your children safe and healthy is one of the worst fears I have ever experienced." In Flint, Michigan, the problem of lead in the water supply was not addressed immediately by the state or federal government, and as a result many children have suffered damage to their brains and nervous systems. Children with lead poisoning can suffer from intellectual disabilities and behavior disorders. High levels of exposure can result in convulsions, coma, and even death.

Take Control of Your Own Water Source

We all take it for granted that when we are thirsty we can simply turn on the tap and fill a glass with clean, fresh drinking water. Let me tell you, there's nothing more shocking or dangerous than when, due to a disaster, contamination, or other emergency, the water is no longer flowing. In *Spy Secrets That Can Save Your Life* I talked about the importance of water storage (as a reminder, the recommended amount of water to keep around is one gallon per person per day—which quickly becomes a large amount of water), since water is obviously essential to survival. So what happens if there's an unexpected emergency and your water source is compromised? You don't want to be fighting over the last gallons of water at Walmart, nor do you want to be stuck in traffic hoping there will be water left for your family by the time you reach the National Guard. While ideally you'll have some containers of water stored in your home to deal with the immediate crisis, what would you do if there were no end in sight? What would you do if you had to find an additional clean water source for your family?

Have a Backup Emergency Water Plan

I highly recommend having an emergency backup plan when it comes to water. If we've learned anything from Flint, Michigan, West Virginia, or hurricanes Katrina and Matthew, it's that we cannot depend on others to provide water during a time of chaos. It's crucial you take measures to protect yourself.

Water Filters

Have a high-quality, easy-to-use filter ready to go: While water storage is important, and you should absolutely aim to have a one-month's water supply for your family, a filter enables you to collect water from almost any natural source. The right filter would allow you to get drinking water from any pond, river, or stream—meaning you would have an unlimited supply.

Identify Local Sources of Water Within Walking Distance

In *Spy Secrets That Can Save Your Life* I talked about the importance of doing HUMINT in your own community—knowing what resources are available in case of an emergency. Noting water sources is part of this process. Always know what streams, rivers, lakes, or ponds are within walking distance in case you ever need to collect water. Having a good filter won't do you any good if you are wandering around searching for a water source. Make sure everyone in your family is aware of the location of these water sources as well.

FAVORITE SPY TOOL: THE BEST WATER FILTER MONEY CAN BUY

My work takes me to some unexpected places for sure. But I never could have imagined that I'd walk into a men's room in a McDonald's where I'd drink the water directly from an unflushed toilet and live to tell about it. I also drank water directly from a scum-filled pond, and out of the absolutely filthy, bug-infested trough the cows drank out of at a livestock auction. What might be even more surprising is that this water went from dark and dirty to clean and fresh in just a few seconds (if it didn't, there's a good chance I would have gotten incredibly sick), and the filter didn't clog. Obviously, access to a clean water supply can mean the difference between life and death, and I wasn't going to recommend a water filter (or risk the lives of my wife and children) without knowing that it truly works.

The water filter I trust my life with is the SurvFilter (www.SurvFilter.com). I keep the SurvFilter in each of my bug-out bags, in my office, in my car, and in the survival kits in my home. The SurvFilter uses nanotechnology and is hands-down the most advanced water filter available. This filter can simply be dropped in a river, lake, stream, etc., and instantly provides clean, safe drinking water. It also has a pump, so you could use this device to clean out a cut on your hand or to fill a water bottle.

TACTIC #2: ARMING YOURSELF IN A WAY THAT WORKS FOR YOU

Protecting Yourself and Your Loved Ones: Improvised Weapons

Whenever I can, I carry a gun—or, if I can't legally carry a gun, a knife. There are times, especially when traveling, when it's not possible to carry either of those. I'm still a big fan of the Tactical Pen I wrote about in *Spy Secrets That Can Save Your Life*. I always carry one with me. You can do some serious damage with this, and it is easy to get through security. I know an individual who got one through the toughest airline security out there—the Israeli airline El Al. And very recently a colleague visiting New York City got it through security at a major tourist attraction. She walked right through with no problem after the woman in front of her was stopped for carrying a sharp object. I've also had clients take the Tactical Pen into the White House. There are many choices of weapons, and it's important to get training and know what you are comfortable using to defend yourself. But what would you do if you suddenly found yourself in a serious situation and you were unarmed? What would you do if someone was trying to snatch your kid off the street or drag you into a van? As always, I urge you to call the police or scream for help before attempting any heroics. However, if your life is truly at stake and you need to fight back, there are some easy-to-make improvised weapons that just might help you get out alive.

PRACTICE AVOIDANCE TO SAVE YOUR LIFE

I can't stress enough how important it is to first try to de-escalate a situation before using self-defense tactics. All of my colleagues would say the same thing—even with decades of combined training using everything from guns and knives to martial arts. We

> Never engage with another person unless it's the only way to save your life.

never forget that even though we are highly trained, we could be coming up against that one person who has better training, or who happens to be out with a bunch of his friends. When your "spidey sense" is up and you feel that something might be about to happen, attempt to avoid the situation and try to go the other way. Avoid saying anything to antagonize the individual further. Never engage with another person unless it's the only way to save your life.

Anything Can Be a Weapon

While I'm going to share some easy ideas for creating weapons, it's also important that you remember that nearly anything can be a weapon. In Raleigh, North Carolina, a twenty-seven-year-old man allegedly kicked down the door to his ex-girlfriend's apartment. He was then stopped in his tracks when he was clobbered over the head with a piece of firewood. If you're working with your laptop in a coffee shop when an attack occurs, you can pick up your laptop and slam it in the attacker's face, causing blunt trauma. Your shoe can work as a weapon—as could a purse, a water bottle, or a flashlight—any hard object. Here are some specific ideas about ordinary items that can be transformed into dangerous weapons:

A SOCK: A regular sock can be used to create a surprisingly powerful weapon. Simply fill the sock with something heavy. Rocks work great, as do golf balls, pool balls, pennies, or even glass ashtrays. Once you've inserted the item or items into the sock, tie a knot at the open end. Now you have a weighted flail, and if you swing it around, you could seriously injure someone. Pro tip: If you are traveling and want to create a weapon using a sock, just buy an ordinary can of soda and stick it inside. (They'll even give you the can when you're on an airplane.)

A SHARP PROJECTILE: A Tactical Pen works well as a projectile. A trip to your local hardware store or Home Depot would also provide lots of options. For example, tent stakes or large nails could be concealed, and then used against an attacker.

KEYS: Replace your key chain with a long strap. This turns your keys into a flail. You could aim to hit someone in the face, distracting him and giving you a chance to run away to safety. You can also use a monkey-fist key chain like I do. It's a paracord key chain with a ball bearing in the middle that can cause serious damage if you hit someone with it.

A PIECE OF PARACORD WITH A METAL NUT TIED TO THE END: This is a surprisingly powerful combination, and it can be worn around the neck for easy access. Just swing the paracord, and the metal nut will definitely hurt someone. We demonstrate how this weapon works in my Spy Escape & Evasion classes, and people are always surprised at how easy it is to crack open a coconut with the nut. The thickness of a coconut is about comparable to that of a human skull, so that gives you a good sense of the injuries you can inflict with this weapon.

THE WEIGHTED BASEBALL CAP: You can sew two sets of ball bearings in the rear of the cap. If you're under attack, just remove the cap and hit the attacker with the part of the cap with the ball bearings.

Whatever weapon you decide to use, remember that your best bet is always to use the weapon to create an opportunity to escape to safety.

FAVORITE SPY TOOL: A STRONG AND LIGHTWEIGHT KNIFE

There's an idea that spies are always walking around with a loaded gun. That might be true sometimes, but it's mostly not. Spies are often sent abroad, in many cases to countries where it is just not possible to carry a gun. A knife is the next best option when it comes to weapons. There's also a practical benefit to a knife. The point of a gun is obviously to stop someone who poses a threat to you. A knife can certainly provide protection, but it can also be useful in a survival situation. A knife can be used to dig, cut through rope, or cut small branches to build a fire or to build a shelter. If you are in a car accident the knife can be used to break the windows so you can get out.

I've been searching for years for the perfect knife, only to be disappointed. My favorite knife is named the NOC, after the most elite and clandestine operatives. This knife is made out of unique, razor-sharp steel, works as a devastating glass-breaking device, and is lightweight. (It's made of the same material used in the aerospace industry and Formula One cars.) It's designed to be nearly unstoppable when slashing, cutting, and doing precision work. It's genuinely everything I've wanted in a knife and it's the ultimate tool for any self-reliant American who wants to be prepared. To see the NOC knife in action (including busting out a car window), visit www.NOCknife.com.

THE MICRO SPY TOOL

This tool has become another favorite with the people who have taken my classes—especially for those individuals who want a way to protect themselves and don't want to carry a gun. The Micro Spy Tool is a discreet and deadly self-defense tool. It's small, easy to conceal, and incredibly sharp. The Micro Spy Tool can be carried in numerous locations, and I've managed to fly with it many times. The shape of the Micro Spy Tool allows you to strike, slash, gouge, and puncture an attacker. The bottom line is, this tool could easily open a major artery.

HOW TO CREATE A SAFE ROOM THAT COSTS ALMOST NOTHING

No one likes to think about what it would be like to experience a home invasion: the terror you would feel waking up in the middle of the night, knowing someone was breaking into your home—and that you and your family were in danger. Or maybe you're enjoying a movie night with your family when someone breaks your front door down. It's not pleasant to think about, and unfortunately this is something that many Americans have experienced.

There are plenty of people out there who will happily build you a state-of-the-art safe room with fortified walls for a hundred thousand dollars or so—and if you have even more to spend, a safe room could easily run into seven figures. Some extremely high-net-worth individuals have been known to install ballistics-proof "safe cores" inside their homes. Some billionaires might build a house with a safe room in mind in the original design. Others hire experts to add a safe room complete with comfortable furniture, a refrigerator, or even a small, full kitchen, air filtration system, and communications equipment. Most of us aren't able to spend that kind of money. Fortunately, it's possible to give your family the benefits of a safe room without going broke. The truth is, you can create something that will work just as well for very little money. A safe room isn't so much about having a bunker to escape to in an emergency as it is about having a predetermined place stocked with supplies where you can gather your family if you are ever attacked. Here's how you can do it.

Choose the Right Room

Choosing the right room is crucial, and there are a few things you should think about when deciding where you want to have your safe room.

Your safe room needs to be located in the room that belongs to the weakest family member. Obviously your six-month-old baby cannot escape out of his room to run to the safe room. You also don't want Grandma to have to climb up the stairs in a hurry. If you have children, plan to designate their room as the safe room (or the room of the youngest child). If you don't have children living in your home, you may want to select a room that's in the interior of your house. If you have a room that has no windows, that could be an excellent option.

Reinforce the Door

Most doors today are hollow and thin—and provide almost nothing in the way of protection. If at all possible, replace hollow doors with solid wood or steel doors that would be much harder to break down. If you want to take things up a notch, consider replacing a wooden doorjamb with a sturdier steel one. This will make it much harder for someone to kick down the door. Make sure there is a high-quality dead bolt on the door to keep out an intruder. Obviously, if you are using a child's room as your safe room you will have to take all the necessary precautions to make sure they don't lock themselves in (or worse, lock you in).

Keep the Room Stocked with Supplies

The idea here is to have a place where your entire family can hide out during a home invasion. However, it's possible you could end up in another type of emergency situation that would require you to remain in the safe room for a longer period of time, such as a riot, a hurricane or other natural disaster, or a major terrorist attack. Be sure to keep your safe room stocked with the following essential items:

- ► Cell phone.
- ► Cell phone charger.
- ► Flashlights.
- ► Batteries.
- ► First-aid kit, medicine (include any prescriptions your family requires as well as painkillers and antibiotics).
- ► Food.
- ► Water.
- ► Additional weapons. (Use whatever weapons work for you. If you are a gun owner, and you opt to keep your gun in someone else's room, always store it in a gun safe.)

Include a Barrier

If possible, it is ideal to have a large, heavy piece of furniture in your safe room. The purpose of this is to have something you and your family can hide behind in the event that shots are fired. You could also hide behind it if you need to shoot back.

PUT YOUR PLAN INTO PRACTICE, AND MASTER IT IN SEVEN SECONDS

Your safe room won't do you any good if you don't have a plan for how to get everyone in it. In *Spy Secrets That Can Save Your Life* I talked about how a thump in the middle of the night (that luckily turned out to be just something falling in a closet) provided an excellent opportunity for me to see that my emergency plan works. If you build a safe room but don't discuss with your family what everyone should do in an emergency, trust me—there will be chaos should the need to use it arise. Talk to your family about what you would like everyone to do if there is a break-in or if the security alarm goes off. Tell the children what to do and where to go. Discuss who is getting the weapon (in my plan, I am the one getting the weapon; I keep my gun loaded in a rapid-access safe on my nightstand for easy access) and who will call for help. Practice your security plan until everyone understands their role and can be inside the safe room within seven seconds.

TACTIC #3: STAYING SAFE IN THE AGE OF INTERNET SHOPPING

Americans are busier than ever, and it's undeniable that Internet shopping makes life a lot easier. You can have just about anything delivered nearly anywhere—from groceries and clothes to gun holsters and pet food. It's become completely normal to shop online, but unfortunately having people bring items to your home brings a threat that most people don't consider.

When Danger Knocks

Lawrence Berry was at his home in Houston with his wife and two daughters when he heard a knock at the door. The holidays were approaching, so when Mr. Berry saw through the door peephole that it was a UPS driver (the individual was dressed in brown), he didn't hesitate to open the door when the man said he needed a signature. Mr. Berry opened the front door, and the "deliveryman" suddenly stuck a gun in his face. The man forced his way inside, and three other armed men appeared and quickly followed. Mr. Berry attempted to grab the gun and got in a tussle with one of the men. The gun discharged and fired bullets into the wall, but thankfully no one was hit. Mr. Berry's wife and two daughters managed to hide in a closet. Mr. Berry was beaten and hit with a stun gun several times. The thieves made off with jewelry and firearms. While this was a horrifying ordeal for Mr. Berry and his family, the end result could have been much, much worse. It's easy to see a brown uniform and think that it's the UPS man. In fact, a colleague of mine once needed to get inside a building for an operation, so he wore all brown and the receptionist automatically assumed he worked for UPS. He got into the building with no questions asked. It would also be easy enough to impersonate a FedEx guy, and keep in mind that extra help around the holidays might not be wearing an official uniform. Amazon hires couriers to deliver items. These individuals drive their own cars, are contract employees, and might be hard to identify. I'm not saying you need to give up having household goods and gifts delivered, but it's important to be vigilant and pay attention to anyone who is approaching your home. Thankfully there are some easy measures you can take to ensure your safety.

Look Beyond the Uniform

The uniform is just one part of the picture, and it's not enough to ensure that the person is in fact a delivery person. Look for other signs that indicate the person is who he says he is. For example, look for the truck and the handheld computer. It won't do you any good to open the door and then ask for an ID if the person intends to do you harm. Have them hold the ID up *before* you open the door.

Don't Sign for Packages

Request that any deliveries be left on your porch (or wherever you want them), and request that a signature not be required. Don't order items that require a signature for delivery.

Have Items Delivered Somewhere Else

I've said it before—I don't have anything delivered to my home, not even pizza. I certainly understand the need to have certain items delivered. However, services like UPS or Federal Express offer options for picking up your items at one of their stores.

Use Technology for Tracking

Shipping services and many retailers offer options for tracking packages and are able to offer frequent and accurate updates. You can track your delivery online or on your phone, and see the precise time and date your package will arrive.

BE CAREFUL ABOUT WHAT YOU PUT IN YOUR TRASH OR RECYCLING

You just bought a new large-screen plasma TV, or maybe you bought a new computer for your kids. You diligently double-check the locks on all your windows and doors nightly, and you always use your alarm. So there's nothing else to worry about, right? Wrong. While, yes, you should always practice good safety measures, don't draw extra attention to your home by essentially announcing to criminals that you have brand-new valuable items in your home. Thieves know that most people just shove the boxes out in the trash—which is like putting up a red flag that you have something new to steal. When you've worked hard and bought yourself a new and expensive item, take the extra time to cut up the box so that it won't be recognizable to criminals.

SPY ENCOUNTERS:
PUT YOUR SECURITY MEASURES INTO PRACTICE EVERYWHERE YOU GO, EVEN IN PARADISE

I highly recommend making a point of practicing your security measures everywhere you go. Don't get lulled into a sense of complacency because you're visiting the hometown you grew up in or you're on vacation. I recently had a wonderful vacation with my family in Hawaii. That vacation in paradise could have turned into a nightmare if I hadn't made a point of practicing my everyday security routine while away from home. The beach was gorgeous, and our house was lovely. The weather was picture-perfect and there was a breeze off the ocean that flowed right into the house. While my wife was putting the kids to bed, I went around the house and closed and locked all the windows. I didn't want to risk having our stuff stolen, or, heaven forbid, someone snatching one of our kids. I noticed that one of the locks was broken. I didn't like this at all, and I set up a "booby trap" so that anyone trying to climb through the window would end up creating a lot of noise that would wake up the entire house. The next morning my brother-in-law came over and said, "Did you hear what happened?" It turned out the house next door was broken into during the night. The thieves slipped in through an unlocked window and stole all their valuables while they were sleeping. At that moment I was so glad I checked our windows, and that I took the time to set up that booby trap, making our house less appealing to thieves.

AS ALWAYS, STAY SAFE AT HOME AND EVERYWHERE YOU GO

It is my wish that after reading this book you feel inspired to think about what actions you can take *right now*—not later, not tomorrow, not next month—to keep you and your family safer. I never want you to be caught off guard or faced with a situation you're not prepared for, so I hope that, like my CIA buddies who are still out in the field, you'll make a point of practicing these tactics until they become second nature to you. Remember that dangerous situations can happen anywhere at any time, so be vigilant at home, at work, at church, at school, and while traveling. Put simply, life is full of many wonderful things and being prepared gives you the peace of mind to enjoy life but also to know you can handle the unpredictable world we live in.

GLOSSARY
OF SPY TERMS

Agent: An individual (usually from a foreign country) who is targeted by the United States, recruited, and trained in the art of tradecraft so that they can provide their country's secrets to the U.S. government.

Asset: A secret source or method. When someone refers to an asset, they are usually referring to an agent.

Bona fides: The proof an individual presents to show they are who they claim to be.

Brush pass: When a case officer and an agent exchange an item, generally by "brushing past" each other in a public place.

Burned: When a case officer's or agent's true identity is compromised.

Case officer: An individual employed by an American intelligence agency whose job is to target individuals (usually from foreign countries), recruit them, teach them tradecraft, and work with them as they provide secret information on behalf of the U.S. government.

Chief of station: The officer who runs a CIA station in a foreign city.

Clandestine operation: An operation meant to be run in secrecy, to be strictly enforced.

Compromised: When it is no longer possible for an agent to remain secret, or for an asset or agent to continue using their cover.

Concealment device: A small item with a secret compartment used to house information that needs to be transferred from one agent to another.

Counterintelligence: The work of keeping tabs on and upsetting the work of foreign intelligence agencies.

Cover: The identity that a case officer is living under while conducting an operation.

Cover stop: A location a case officer or agent would enter along a surveillance detection route (SDR), such as a store or restaurant, to give the impression to those following him that he is behaving normally.

Covert operation: A secret operation undertaken by a government against a foreign state. Such operations are planned and executed in a manner that any participation by the government perpetrating them will be denied.

Dead drop: A location where a concealment device is left by one agent for another to retrieve.

HUMINT: Intelligence that is collected from human sources.

Hunker-down site: A location, usually predetermined by an agent, where he can hide safely until a perceived threat has passed.

Intrusion point: A location that an agent who believes he is under surveillance can enter in order to lead the individual to follow the agent inside.

Krypto: An alias used by a case officer or agent.

Legal traveler: An individual who may have citizenship or the legal right to reside in one country, while holding a passport or visa that enables him to easily travel to another country.

Narco-terrorist: A drug dealer or drug king known for inflicting terrible abuse on those who work with him.

Safe house: Any hotel room, apartment, or house that is deemed "safe" by intelligence officers. It may be used to hold clandestine meetings or to house agents during an operation.

Signal: A secret method of communication used between an agent and a case officer, often to indicate to each other that a preplanned meeting should or should not take place.

Surveillance detection route (SDR): A route, which could be short or even hours or days long, that a case officer or agent takes to ensure that he himself is not under surveillance.

REFERENCES

Banjo, Shelly. "Home Depot Hackers Exposed 53 Million Email Addresses." *Wall Street Journal*, November 6, 2014.

Bernstein, Lenny. "What It's Like to Die of Thirst." Washingtonpost.com, August 7, 2014.

Bertrand, Natasha. "Here's What Happened to Your Target Data That Was Hacked." *Business Insider*, October 20, 2014.

Brennan, Morgan. "Billionaire Bunkers: Beyond the Panic Room, Home Security Goes Sci-Fi." *Forbes*, December 12, 2013.

Burkett, Randy. "An Alternative Framework for Agent Recruitment: From MICE to RASCLS." *Studies in Intelligence* 57, no. 1 (2013): 7–17.

"CONTACT 13: Thieves Dress up as UPS Workers." KTNV, December 4, 2016.

Crimesider Staff. "Cops: Slain Realtor Was to Show Home to Murder Suspect." CBS News, September 30, 2014.

Crimesider Staff. "Police: Babysitter's Abuse of Child Caught on 'Nanny Cam.'" CBS News, January 1, 2016.

Cunningham, Erin. "In Their Latest Outrage, Islamic State Fighters Are Using Water as a Weapon in Iraq." *Washington Post*, October 7, 2014.

Ford, Dana. "Risky Business: Real Estate Agent's Killing Hits Home for Realtors." CNN, October 1, 2014.

Gabriel, Trip. "Thousands Without Water After Spill in West Virginia." Nytimes.com, January 10, 2014.

Gerken, James. "On the Anniversary of the Elk River Chemical Spill, West Virginians Tell Their Stories." TheHuffingtonPost.com, January 9, 2015.

Giordono, Joseph. "New Army Program Aims to Put Soldiers on Higher Alert for IEDs." *Stars and Stripes*, n.p., May 25, 2005.

Hammond, Jeffrey, and Leonard Cole. "Epidemiology of Terrorism Injuries." In Shmuel Shapira, *Essentials of Terror Medicine*. New York: Springer Science & Business Media, 2008, p. 157.

"Home Health Aide Caught on Camera Abusing 78-Year-Old Stroke Victim." NBC New York, December 30, 2016.

"Husband of California Mom Kidnapped While Jogging Reveals Details of Her Ordeal." *Fox News*, November 29, 2016.

Marcus, Lillet. "9/11 'Hero Dog' Saved Woman Trapped in Rubble for 27 Hours." TODAY.com, September 13, 2013.

Meltzer, Matt. "7 Countries Where You're Most Likely to Get Kidnapped." *Thrillist*, n.p., November 23, 2016. Web. 01 Dec. 2016.

Musumeci, Natalie. "How This Home Intruder Got What He Deserved." *New York Post*, n.p., December 28, 2016.

"Nanny Cam Caught Alleged Abuse by California Babysitter." ABC11, March 4, 2016.

Prideaux, Eric. "Shades of Sunakku." *Japan Times RSS*, n.p., February 14, 2004.

Shontell, Alyson. "Miss Teen USA Was 'In Tears and Shock' After a Hacker Took Nude Photos Through Her Bedroom Webcam." *Business Insider*, May 23, 2014.

Wagner, Meg. "Kidnapped Calif. Mom Sherri Papini Still Chained When Found." *NY Daily News*, n.p., December 1, 2016.

Williams, David K. "What a Fighter Pilot Knows About Business: The OODA Loop." *Forbes*, February 9, 2013.

Workman, Karen, Eli Rosenberg, and Christopher Mele. "Chelsea Bombing: What We Know and Don't Know." *New York Times*, September 20, 2016.

Zetter, Kim. "Teen Who Hacked CIA Director's Email Tells How He Did It." *Wired*, October 19, 2015.

Zetter, Kim. "Tools of Tradecraft: The CIA's Historic Spy Kit." *Wired*, November 2, 2011.

ACKNOWLEDGMENTS

I'm grateful to my fellow CIA officers who contributed their stories to this book. Our nation is blessed for your service and for your willingness to put your lives on the line for our country.

ABOUT THE AUTHOR

Jason R. Hanson is a former CIA Officer and security specialist. His Spy Escape & Evasion firm has trained thousands of Americans in critical safety and survival skills. Jason is a frequent media guest and has appeared on *The Today Show, Dateline, Rachael Ray, Shark Tank, Fox & Friends*, and more. He's also the *New York Times* best-selling author of *Spy Secrets That Can Save Your Life*. Jason resides in Cedar City, Utah, with his family.